THE DREAM INTERPRETATION HANDBOOK

HANDBOOK

A GUIDE & DICTIONARY TO UNLOCK THE MEANINGS OF YOUR DREAMS

Karen Frazier

ALTHEA
PRESS

For Tanner and Abby as they begin their new lives together

For general information on our other products and services or to obtain technical support, please contact our Customer Care Department within the United States at (866) 744-2665, or outside the United States at (510) 253-0500.

Althea Press publishes its books in a variety of electronic and print formats. Some content that appears in print may not be available in electronic books, and vice versa.

Interior and Cover Designer: Rachel Haeseker
Art Producer: Sue Bischofberger
Editor: Nana K. Twumasi
Production Manager: Holly Haydash
Production Editor: Melissa Edeburn

Author photo courtesy of © Tristan David Luciotti

ISBN: Print 978-1-64152-284-7 | eBook 978-1-64152-285-4

CONTENTS

INTRODUCTION

I've always been a vivid dreamer. As a child, my dreams were so intense I would sometimes wake up confused about which world was real: my dream world, or the one where I found myself tucked snugly under the covers in my bedroom. Once, following a particularly vivid dream in which I was a different person living in a completely different place, I got out of my bed, walked downstairs to my parents' bedroom, and told them I was ready to go home. I was furious when they insisted that I was already home, and reluctantly trudged back to bed.

As I got older, my intense dreams continued. In college, I decided I needed to figure out not only why I had such powerful dreams but also what the dreams meant. I had a feeling they were trying to tell me something important, and I wanted to uncover what it was.

Fortunately, college attendance came with an all-access pass to the comprehensive university library where I checked out every book on dreams I could get my hands on. I also took a class in dream interpretation through the school's psychology department. Through the class and my own reading, I became acquainted with Sigmund Freud, Carl Jung, Calvin S. Hall, Jr., and others with theories on dreams. The more I learned, the more passionate I became about the power of dream interpretation.

Over the past 30 years, I've continued my exploration into the world of dreams. When I found classes, I immediately signed up. When I discovered new books, I devoured them. Most importantly, I interpreted my own dreams. I discovered that, regardless of what is going on in my life, my dreams always offer valuable insight into my subconscious mind, put me in touch with my emotions, help me realize unrecognized ambitions, and show me any unacknowledged pain. The content of my dreams opens new spiritual pathways, offers me a way forward during difficult times, and encourages me to find ways to heal those parts of me that are hurting.

As you might imagine, the ability to interpret dreams makes for a great conversation starter. When my friends discovered that I was able to do it, they started asking me about their dreams. From recurring dreams about not having studied for finals, to deeply frightening apocalyptic dreams, I've heard them all! I've interpreted hundreds of dreams for others and myself, both in person and through the dream interpretation column I write for *Paranormal Underground* magazine. My ultimate goal, however, is to teach others to find the meaning in their own dreams. To do this, I turned the way I interpret dreams into a system that I teach in classes and at national conferences.

This book is built around my dream interpretation system and also offers a basis to understand why we dream, what types of dreams we have, and when we should pay attention to them because they might be telling us something. It relies on my years of study as well as work with dream and psychic symbols, psychological archetypes, and dream interpretation for myself and others.

If you're new to the practice of dream interpretation, dream dictionaries—like the one in part 2 of this book (see page 77)—offer a great place to start. You can also find dream dictionaries that define hundreds, if not thousands, of terms and symbols, and I encourage you to use one or more along with the process I teach here. To get you started, I've included definitions of the 100 most common dream symbols you're likely to encounter. What this book offers, however, goes beyond a basic dream dictionary. It will teach you to recognize the type of dreams you have and decide which are worthy of interpretation. Then, you'll learn my step-by-step process for interpreting your dreams using context, universal dream symbols, intuition, and personal symbolism that can't be found in any dream dictionary.

I encourage you to start using these tools as soon as possible. Don't worry if you feel you're doing it "wrong"; practicing is the best way to learn. When my students start to use the process, they are often surprised at just how accurately their dreams address ongoing issues in their lives and how those dreams can offer guidance. You can experience this, too, if you allow it. I am humbled and grateful you have chosen me to guide you on this journey to discover the secret life of your dreams.

HOW TO USE THIS BOOK

This book has two parts. In part 1, chapter 1, I discuss the history of dream interpretation from ancient to modern times. I also explore the many theories from key players in psychological, spiritual, and cognitive dream interpretation, including Freud, Jung, and Hall. You'll discover why we dream and the various types of dreams we have, and you'll learn some key features of each type of dream so you can discern if a dream is worthy of interpretation. We'll take a look at the spiritual basics of dream interpretation as well, discussing how symbolism in dreams can come from various spiritual traditions and cultures, and how understanding dreams can lead to spiritual, personal, and emotional growth.

In chapter 2, we'll discuss common dream contexts—or types—and how the meaning behind the context of your dreams is one of the main keys to their interpretation.

In chapter 3, I outline the step-by-step process I created for interpreting dreams. You'll learn which dream elements are symbolic and how to discern their meaning based not only on the universal symbolism found in

dream dictionaries, but also the personal symbolism in your life. (This personal symbolism arises from the personal unconscious as well as individual, familial, spiritual, and cultural symbols from your unique background.) You'll also learn how to connect these symbols to your life in a meaningful way to better understand what your subconscious is trying to tell you through your dreams. To further assist you, I walk you through several dream interpretations I have done and show you how I applied my process to come up with that interpretation.

In part 2, you'll find a dictionary of the 100 most common dream symbols. When I teach classes, write my column, and give lectures, I see the same symbols over and over again. If they come up in so many other people's dreams, chances are they arise in yours as well. These symbols often have common associations that come from the collective consciousness, a repository of symbols shared by humanity described by Carl Jung.

It's important to note that if you read three different dream dictionaries, you'll find that each has its own interpretation for dream symbols that differs slightly from the others. This has been a source of confusion for people who take my dream interpretation class. Therefore, in the definitions for each term, I help you understand the basis for the interpretation to minimize confusion when working with different dictionaries.

One final thought before we get started: Just as there's no wrong way to interpret your dreams, there's no wrong way to use this book. I encourage you to read the first three chapters for background and the steps to dream interpretation before you dive into the dictionary so you have a strong foundation. That said, I completely understand if you're eager to get straight into decoding your dreams. In that case, you can jump right to the process in chapter 3, but be sure to reference part 2 for the dream symbols and chapter 2 for the dream contexts. Whichever method you choose, remember that dreams are deeply personal and always keep your intuition at the fore. Sometimes an interpretation feels right, even if it's not the exact meaning a dream dictionary suggests. With an open mind and your dream interpretation tools at hand—dream journal, dream dictionary, and my interpretation process—you'll always be ready to delve into a dream.

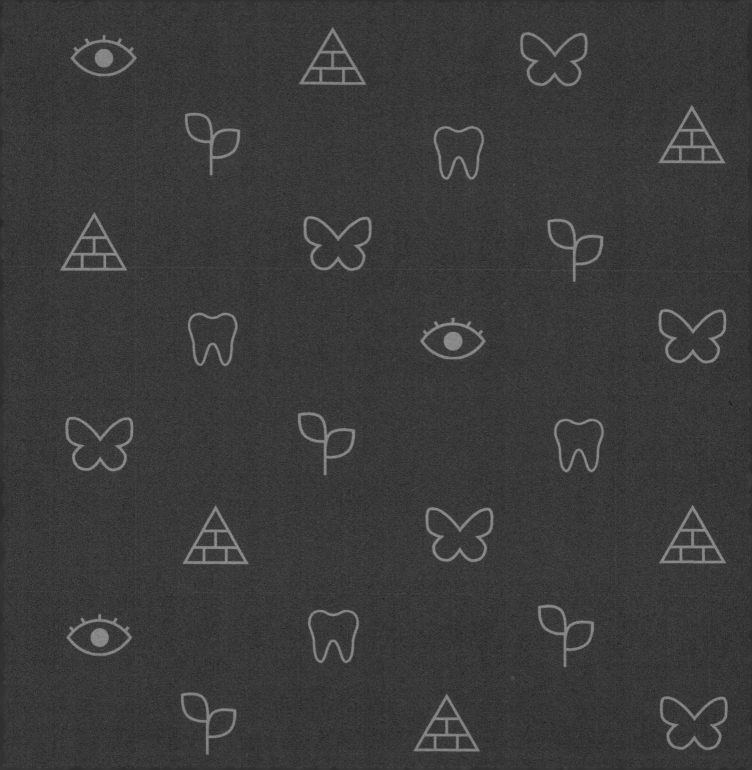

Part I
INTERPRETING
DREAMS

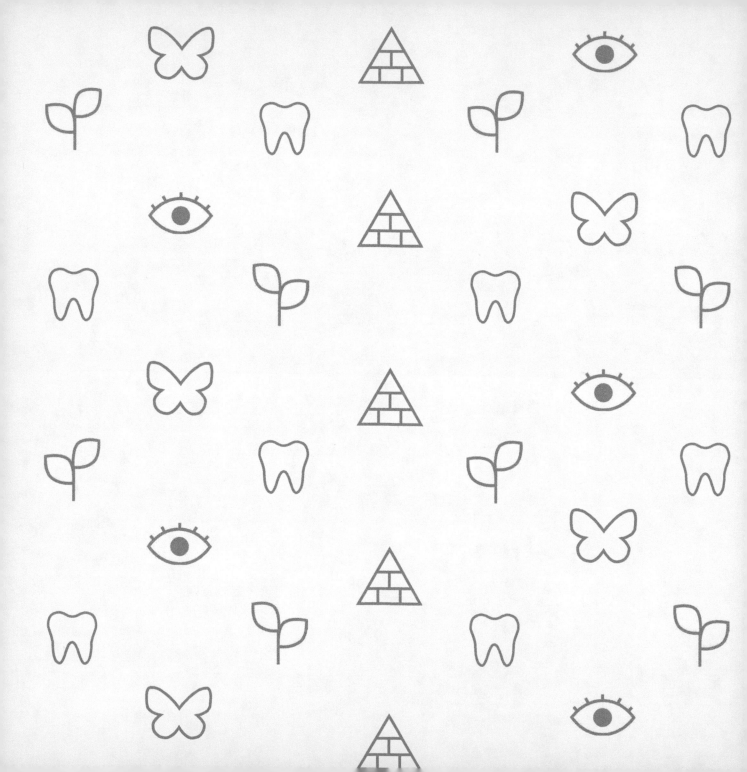

CHAPTER ONE

ON DREAMING: THE SPIRITUAL AND THE SCIENTIFIC

Dreams have fascinated people for thousands of years. Even ancient civilizations sought to discover why they dreamed and what meaning existed in the strange visions they had while they slept. However, it wasn't until the turn of the twentieth century when Sigmund Freud wrote *The Interpretation of Dreams* that dreams became the subject of formal study.

In this chapter, I share background information about dream interpretation, from ancient Egyptian approaches and beliefs to thoroughly modern methods. We'll discuss the religious and spiritual foundations for dream interpretation as well as the purely practical. This background is important if you wish to become proficient at interpreting your dreams—each philosophy contains truths and wisdom you can call upon as you seek to discover the meaning of your dreams.

Dreaming has been so effective for me in this way that every night before I go to sleep, I say, "Tell me what I need to know."

WHY WE DREAM

Dreams are experiences you have when you're asleep. Dreaming occurs when your ego (your sense of self) shuts down and you are in a state of sleep known as rapid eye movement (REM). At this point your body isn't moving but your brain is still sending out signals as if it is—which is likely what allows you to dream. According to research at the University of California Santa Barbara, when you dream, you *experience* it as opposed to *watching* it like a movie. You're right in the center of the action and, for the time you are unconscious, the experience feels very real. It evokes real emotions and you experience physical sensations in your dreams. On average, a person has four to six dreams a night, according to the National Sleep Foundation.

Psychology Today points out that the reasons for dreaming are still poorly understood by science and, in fact, some scientists believe dreams serve no purpose whatsoever. Others, however, feel dreams do serve various purposes ranging from the mundane to the spiritual. Here's a look at some of the benefits dreams may bring us.

Memory Sorting

According to an article in *Current Biology*, one of the main functions of dreaming is memory processing, which basically means sorting memories into specific spots in your brain. This occurs during sleep, when sensory input is at a minimum, so the brain is free to sort memory fragments from the day and move them to long-term storage. These dreams tend to be mundane and unmemorable.

Neurological Maintenance

In 1977, two Harvard University psychiatrists, J. Allan Hobson and Robert W. McCarley, posited that dreams are caused by neuron activity that occurs during REM sleep. This arises from the natural chemical shift that occurs during the transition between waking and sleeping. These chemicals stimulate brain activity, causing memory fragments to surface as dreams. This is called the "activation-synthesis" hypothesis.

Wish Fulfillment

Sigmund Freud hypothesized that dreaming was a form of wish fulfillment. According to Freud's work, *The Interpretation of Dreams* (see more later in this chapter), dreaming satisfies unconscious desires from our waking life.

Extending Our Waking Life

Some people also see dreaming as an extension of waking life. This is particularly true of lucid dreaming or astral projection dreams, where dreamers feel consciously unconscious during REM sleep and actively control the content of their dreams.

Enhancing Creativity

One of the things many people believe—me included—is that dreaming seems to enhance creativity. I often see creative ideas during my sleep and then wake and act on them. Science seems to back this up. For example, a study published in *Proceedings of the National Academy of Sciences* showed that REM sleep and dreaming improved associative networks, which can help find creative solutions to problems. This can also benefit creative pursuits such as art, music, and writing. Singer/songwriter Paul McCartney has related that the words to the hit song "Yesterday" came up in a dream. Likewise, I've dreamed entire articles, content for my books, and blog posts.

Working Through Our Problems

I also use dreaming as a form of problem solving. In fact, dreaming has been so effective for me in this way that every night before I go to sleep, I say, "Tell me what I need to know." If I have a specific problem I'm trying to solve, I may specifically ask about that issue. For instance, I might say before I go to sleep, "Tell me what I need to know about my marriage," or "Tell me what I need to know about teaching this class." I often wake in the morning having worked through my problem subconsciously during dreams. For example, I may understand that my husband and I aren't hearing what the other is saying, or I might have an idea for a new activity I can introduce in one of my classes.

Messages from the Subconscious, Higher Self, or Spirit

Carl Jung popularized the theory that dreams are messages from the subconscious, whereas psychic Edgar Cayce suggested dreams contained messages from the higher self with symbolism arising from the collective consciousness. In fact, Cayce suggested dreams could tell the dreamer anything one needed to know about oneself.

I wholeheartedly believe that dreaming sends us valuable messages from both our own subconscious and from our spirit guides. Spirit guides are those beings in the spiritual realm that provide prompting as we walk a spiritual path as humans. Many of my dreams contain profound messages that guide me along my spiritual path. Take, for instance, when I first met my husband. He felt familiar to me, but I didn't think I liked him very much. Then I had a dream encouraging me to get to know him, so I did. We are now approaching our eighteenth year together. If I'd relied on my first instinct instead of heeding my dream, I likely would have never taken the time to get to know him.

Visits from the Dead

If you've ever had a dream in which you spend time with someone who has passed, then you've likely experienced a visitation dream and understand how powerful they can be. Visitation dreams are common. Many experts and psychic mediums believe they occur because, during the dream state, the dreamer's defenses are down, so it's the easiest way for someone who has died to send direct messages of love. Boston University neurology professor Patrick McNamara notes these dreams are common, widespread, and have similar qualities among dreamers that differentiate them from other types of dreams.

My own dreams in which loved ones who have passed visit me are so vivid and powerful that I wake feeling as if I just spent time with that person. I can still recall a series of visitation dreams that had a big impact on me. I once dreamed about the partner of an old friend several nights in a row. I hadn't seen either person for years but I knew the partner had died recently. At first, I just thought it was odd that I was dreaming about him but didn't assign much significance to it—until after several nights in the dream he said, "Tell her!" I contacted my friend and told her about what I had dreamed. There were significant details in the dreams with information she and her daughter needed to hear in order to heal from a deeply profound loss.

To Tell Us Something about Ourselves

Perhaps the most important reason for dreaming is that, if we are willing to listen to and interpret our dreams, they tell us something about ourselves. These are usually messages about our tendencies, habits, beliefs, and emotions as opposed to the messages we receive from our higher selves and guides about our spiritual path. Dreams often contain symbolic elements that help us get to know what lurks in our subconscious. Acknowledging these aspects of ourselves that hide in the shadows can help us heal and move forward in a more empowered and integrated manner.

Take, for example, a dream I once had about a talking kangaroo unaware that he was a kangaroo, dressed like a detective. In the dream, I kept trying to help the kangaroo identify that it was, indeed, a kangaroo, but he was having none of it. My interpretation: The dream was showing me how I often need to project my own "label" onto others based on preconceived notions instead of allowing them to show me who they are.

ANCIENT INTERPRETATIONS

The concept of dream interpretation has existed for thousands of years, spanning multiple civilizations. You'll find examples of our fascination with dreams extending into antiquity. Many early cultures believed dreams were divinatory in nature, although the significance varied for each.

Babylonia/Mesopotamia

Accounts of dream analysis in Mesopotamia date back more than 5,000 years, to 3100 BCE. Early Mesopotamian texts often contained accounts of dreams, particularly those of royalty, according to an analysis by Curtiss Hoffman in the journal *Dreaming*.

The Mesopotamians used dream analysis as a form of divination and they acted on the messages they believed their dreams contained. For example, Gudea (2144 to 2124 BCE), ruler of the Sumerian city-state of Lagash, rebuilt a temple to the war god Ningirsu after having a dream instructing him how to do so.

Likewise, the ancient poem *Epic of Gilgamesh*, which dates back to about 2100 BCE, relays various dreams and interpretations. Most of the dreams described in the poem symbolically foreshadowed events that would occur in Gilgamesh's life. Gilgamesh's friend Enkidu interprets many dreams throughout the epic. In one dream, a mountain falls on them, which Enkidu interprets as the defeat of Humbaba, the guardian of a forbidden cedar forest through which Gilgamesh and Enkidu are traveling.

Ancient Egypt

The ancient Egyptians also believed that dreams foretold the future. An Egyptian papyrus dating from the 1200s BCE was acquired from a family near Deir el-Medina, who had passed it down through generations. It is considered an Egyptian dream book. The papyrus starts, "If a man sees himself in a dream . . ." and then lists various dreams and indicates whether they are "good" or "bad" omens. It describes more than 100 different dreams and lists symbols and actions that may appear in the dreams, suggesting Egyptians recognized the symbolic nature of the content of dreams.

Writer Anita Stratos notes that these dreams focused on commoners, not royalty, suggesting dream interpretation was part of regular life in ancient Egypt.

Ancient Greece

Ancient Greek mythology included an entire family of gods dedicated to sleep and dreams, including Hypnos, the god of sleep; his son Morpheus, the god of dreams; and Morpheus's brother, Phobetor, the personification of nightmares. Morpheus and the Oneiroi (deities that controlled dreams) appeared in Ovid's *Metamorphoses*, written in the eighth century CE.

The ancient Greeks believed the content of dreams was significant. In fact, the first known book of dream interpretation came from a fourth-century BCE Greek named Antiphon, offering a practical guide to interpreting and understanding dreams. In the second century CE, another Greek author named Artemidorus wrote a similar treatise called *Oneirocritica*. Artemidorus suggested two types of dreams: a continuation of daily activities during the sleep state that examined the recent past, and prophetic dreams that foretold the future.

Detailing a Dream: Aiko

In the next few chapters, I will detail dreams others have sent to me. The first few will be without comment, just to give you a feel for the dreams and their interpretations. In later chapters I will detail dreams and describe how I arrived at the interpretation. If you'd like to follow along with the interpretive process or try to determine how I arrived at the interpretation, the process is in chapter 3, and the dream dictionary is at the end of the book (see page 77).

Aiko's Dream

Aiko dreamed she was a nurse at a hospital. Arriving at work, she put on her scrubs in the locker room. The scrubs were a dirty green and she also put on a plastic butcher's apron. She put her stethoscope around her neck—not into her ears. She went to the ward in which she worked where she saw another nurse in tidy, forest-green scrubs. Suddenly, Aiko felt dirty and disheveled compared to the other nurse. Aiko wanted to change and get the right scrubs but something prevented it.

Interpretation

Hospitals in dreams represent healing, so this dream is about healing or health.

★ Nurse means being a healer or needing healing

★ Scrubs represent the desire to clean up one's act

★ Green represents health and positive changes; muddy green suggests ambivalence about the changes

★ Apron represents protection and secrecy

★ Stethoscope represents listening; however, Aiko mentions she isn't using it to listen, suggesting she may be unwilling to hear a message

★ Scrubs a clearer green than Aiko's suggest she feels inadequate but wants to change that

★ Being unable to change scrubs suggests Aiko feels something prevents her from meeting her aspirations

Aiko's dream suggests she is trying to heal some aspect of herself, but something is preventing it. She either is not hearing the information she receives, or is hearing it but interpreting it incorrectly and she's being overly self-protective. This makes Aiko feel unworthy, but she wants to change.

You can also glean an idea of how dreams were viewed in ancient Greece by looking at the ideas of the philosophers of the day. Hippocrates believed dreams could foretell physical illnesses. Aristotle believed dreams could be prophetic. Plato suggested dreamers acted out guilty acts in their sleep that they would not normally do while awake.

Ancient China

The ancient Chinese beliefs in dream interpretation arose from the concept of Taoism. Taoists believed dreams could offer lessons and that dreams were just another state of being. The whole person was a combination of both their unconscious dreaming state and their conscious waking one. The Chinese also believed dream states were not hallucinations but, rather, alternate realities that occurred when one was asleep.

DIVINE DREAMS

Dream interpretation even appears in the Bible. Several times in the Old Testament, dream interpretation is mentioned, such as in Genesis 40, which tells the story of the Pharaoh's cupbearer and baker who were imprisoned with Joseph—both had the same dream on the same night. When Joseph spoke to them, they told him of their matching dreams. "They said to him, 'We have had dreams, and there is no one to interpret them.'" Joseph interpreted their dreams, telling the cupbearer his dream meant the Pharaoh would restore him to his position within three days; the baker's dream meant Pharaoh would execute him.

Earlier in the book of Genesis, a teenaged Joseph recounted two dreams: one in which bundles of grain his brothers had gathered bowed down to his bundles of grains, and one in which the Sun, Moon, and stars bowed down to Joseph. Threatened, Joseph's brothers conspired to kill him. They stripped off his coat of many colors and sold him into slavery. Later, Joseph became a powerful adviser to the Pharaoh when he was able to interpret his many dreams. Genesis is careful to point out, however, that the gift of dream interpretation was God's, not Joseph's.

Later, a similar story plays out in the second chapter of the book of Daniel. In it, Daniel interprets King Nebuchadnezzar's dream in which he saw a statue made from four metals.

God supplied Daniel with both the contents of the king's dream and an interpretation, and Daniel went to the king and explained what his dream was and what it meant. Nebuchadnezzar was so impressed by Daniel's interpretation he raised Daniel to a high position as an adviser in his kingdom.

These two stories are just a sample of many instances of dream interpretation present in the Bible. However, they illustrate an important history found in the Bible in which God supplied the content of dreams to certain people as visions or a way of communicating messages. According to the United Church of God, God can communicate through dreams; however, it isn't his normal method of communication. This type of communication is rare and some dreams may be attempts from spirits to mislead the faithful.

Other faiths also have their own beliefs about dreams. For instance, in the Islamic faith it is believed that there are three types of dreams: true dreams, dreams where one is speaking to oneself, and a dream from *Shaytaan* (Satan) in an attempt to frighten the dreamer. Those people with disturbing dreams are counseled to seek refuge with Allah.

Before he was enlightened, Buddha had seven highly symbolic dreams that, when interpreted, foretold of his coming enlightenment. However, Buddha was skeptical about dreams, believing they were part of the process of the mind as opposed to divinely inspired. Buddha forbade monks from interpreting dreams because he was also skeptical of one's ability to interpret the dreams of others. The official Buddhist belief is that dreams come from the mind, not the Divine, but they can have psychological significance or reveal something about the dreamer.

As you can see, dream interpretation is significant in many faiths, often attributed to God or inspiration from God. I believe my own dreams are sometimes inspired by my higher self, my guides, or source energy. If you come from a particular faith, you're welcome to invite that understanding and belief into your dream interpretation. However, I do not offer interpretation tools based on any particular faith or religion.

Motivated Reasoning

Also known as emotion-based decision making, motivated reasoning is a cognitive theory suggesting humans deceive themselves in their decision-making process by rationalizing their choices based on their biases and emotions.

Emotion-based decision making arises from ego and perceiving the world through our ego-based filters. Everyone has emotional, cognitive, and experiential filters in place, which are influenced by the need to be seen and to see ourselves as good people. When our choices or behaviors are out of character with our self-image, cognitive dissonance occurs. To resolve this dissonance, we rationalize our own choices, even if those choices or actions are things we would not condone in others.

For example, suppose your philosophy is to treat others as you'd like to be treated and always be kind. Yet, one day, someone cuts you off in traffic and, after calling them a few choice names, you flip them the bird. This clearly goes against your stated ethic of treating others as you'd like to be treated; however, you are able to rationalize this behavior by saying that person deserved the reaction because their behavior warranted it.

The subconscious sees through these filters, understanding the real "I" of who we are beyond all the false identities we project to maintain our sense of self. Dreaming is inherently self-aware, as the subconscious provides a reflection of you beyond your ego. Dreams reveal the fallacy of the face we present in the world, drawing attention to the shadow-self (the parts of ourselves we would prefer to disown because they don't fit our self-image) we hide from using motivated reasoning.

Seeing beyond filters is essential to live our most authentic lives. Dreams hold up a mirror to our true self and challenge us to meet our shadows, integrating them into our waking lives.

FREUDIAN DREAMS

No discussion of modern dream interpretation is complete without the modern father of dream interpretation, Sigmund Freud. Freud is credited with developing psychoanalysis, a tool still used today. Psychoanalysis seeks to treat mental or emotional issues by exploring the interaction between the subconscious and conscious mind to discover repressed thoughts, beliefs, emotions, and fears. Dream interpretation figured significantly into Freud's theories and techniques of psychoanalysis. It was the first time dreams were tied into human psychology and used in a way that revealed the psyche of the dreamer.

The Interpretation of Dreams

In 1900 Sigmund Freud published *The Interpretation of Dreams* (*Die Traumdeutung* in German), his treatise on dream analysis. The book is essentially the history of dream interpretation, as Freud believed dreams could be used in his method of psychoanalysis. Now, more than a century later, some of Freud's theories hold up, whereas others have been refined or disputed by those who came after him.

Freud believed his theory of dreaming revealed the secrets of dreams that philosophers and dreamers had sought for thousands of years. He began working on his theory after a dream he had in July 1895, which he called "Irma's injection." It was about a patient of Freud's who, after Freud's treatment, continued to get sicker. Freud believed he used the content of his dream to relieve himself of any mistakes he had made in his care leading to Irma's worsening condition, which led him to theorize his dream was a form of wish fulfillment designed to make him feel better about a real-life patient to whom he might have offered better care.

After his dream about Irma and his subsequent analysis of it, Freud began working on *The Interpretation of Dreams*. Based on his own dream and those his patients shared with him, Freud concluded dreams must exist as a form of wish fulfillment, in which the dreamer resolved problems in a manner that met one's deepest wishes and desires.

Wish Fulfillment

Freud believed dreams, fantasies, daydreams, and delusions all represented unfulfilled wishes. He believed people had many wishes (frequently arising from unfulfilled sexual urges) they repressed because they found those desires inappropriate or unconscionable. One example Freud used was the Oedipus complex, in which Freud believed a child wanted the love of their opposite sex parent to be theirs alone, thus, unconsciously, desiring the death of the other parent. Dreams, then, revealed these unconscious urges.

The Interpretive Process

Freud divided dream content into two categories:

Manifest content: This includes things that appear in dreams that the dreamer can consciously remember upon waking. The parts of your dreams you recall, such as symbols, actions, people, and other details are all the manifest content of the dream.

Latent content: According to Freud, the latent content of the dream includes all the things the dreamer doesn't know consciously. This includes the subconscious meanings of the dream driven by unconscious desires, drives, and needs as well as the symbols that represent these things in the dreamer's subconscious mind. It reveals the dreamer's true motivations, even if they are unknown to the dreamer in the waking world. Freud believed interpreting this latent content could reveal the dreamer to himself.

Freud believed the process for interpreting dreams was best achieved through free association. In this process, the interpreter provides the meaning of symbols in the dream to the dreamer, while the dreamer uses free association to try to understand what the symbols are saying about their subconscious. He also believed our minds substituted symbols for distasteful objects in dreams to make those objects more palatable to the dreamer. For example, he believed a train represented a phallus and the train entering a tunnel represented intercourse. Likewise, he said death in dreams was represented by going on a journey, thus replacing something distasteful (death) with something acceptable (travel).

Freud also theorized dreams relayed information through various mechanisms, including the following:

Projection: In projection, the dreamer projects their desires or negative traits onto others in the dream. For example, if someone is criticizing you in a dream, it may be you projecting your self-criticism onto another.

Displacement: According to Freud, when something that has been repressed comes back in a disguised way in the content of a dream, it's a type of displacement. This is a form of distortion. In a dream, an example of displacement might be getting angry with a person for some minor infraction that you, yourself, have committed in waking life.

Symbolism: As previously mentioned, Freud also believed symbols appeared in dreams to substitute for items, beliefs, or other things

the dreamer found distasteful, such as the previously mentioned train or journey.

Condensation: What is repressed can often appear in hidden ways in dreams. For example, two or more experiences or ideas are condensed into a single symbol or action in a dream, and interpreting it can reveal the repressed emotions or events. An example of this might be a person who appears in your dream who is a composite of both your parents.

Rationalization: This is the final key to Freud's beliefs about the meaning of dreams. It is a process in which the content from the dream, with its subconscious symbols and cues, is reorganized into a dream that has meaning to the dreamer.

Pioneers of the Psychological Approach to Dreams

Many others followed Freud in his psychoanalytic approach to dream interpretation.

Carl Jung

Next to Freud's, Jung's is probably the most well-known theory of dream interpretation. Freud and Jung were friends and they often shared and discussed their differing views of psychoanalysis and dream interpretation. Jung was younger than Freud and he dismissed some of Freud's approach to dreams (particularly Freud's tendency to see sex in everything), but he built on other aspects of it to create a theory of dream interpretation that was both psychological and mystical.

Like Freud, Jung believed dreams were symbolic in nature, but he didn't buy into the notion that dreams were a form of wish fulfillment. Instead, Jung believed the symbolic nature of dreams was fluid based on experience and beliefs and that certain dreams were archetypal in nature, showing representations of one's true nature through personal and universal symbolism and the appearance of archetypes, or overarching universal themes.

Calvin S. Hall, Jr.

Calvin S. Hall, Jr. was a student of both Freudian and Jungian dream interpretation. In the early 1950s Hall developed his own theory of dream interpretation that was cognitive in its approach, arguing dreams were a result of cognitive (thinking) processes as opposed to harboring some deep psychological meaning (see more on Hall on page 48).

Ann Faraday

In the 1970s, British doctoral student Ann Faraday did her dissertation research at London's University College studying dreams. Her research findings, which she published in books such as *The Dream Game*, helped popularize the idea of interpreting dreams based on their symbolism. She provided a way for laypeople to interpret their own dreams.

David Foulkes

David Foulkes directs a dream research laboratory at the University of Wyoming and another at the Georgia Mental Health Institute. Through his research, Foulkes has determined that the content of dreams is more realistic and mundane than it is fantastical, and dream imagery is realistic and plausible; thus, new theories of dream interpretation and imagery are needed. He believes dream thought processes are not dissimilar to waking thought processes and, therefore, one should think about dreaming in different ways from earlier forms of dream interpretation, which could lead to new ideas about dreams and their meanings.

Edgar Cayce

Edgar Cayce was not a psychologist or researcher but, in fact, a famous psychic. However, a discussion of dream interpretation pioneers isn't complete without at least mentioning him. Cayce believed the content of dreams revealed our inner selves and our higher vision and desires. He also believed dreams could be prophetic and diagnostic, offering their messages in symbolism that came from the collective consciousness. This approach, a hybrid of psychology and mysticism, is still used by many to interpret their dreams.

Dream-Work

In Freudian psychoanalysis, dream-work is the process in which the dreamer and psychoanalyst delve into the contents of dreams and the ideas, thoughts, and images the dreams evoke to serve as a basis for deeper analysis. Because dreamers have their own imagery or "language," this varies from person to person. Freud believed hidden desires were distorted and reappeared in dreams in veiled ways. Dream-work served to resolve this conflict and reveal the dreamer to oneself.

For example, if someone dreams of going on a hike and is excited to be out in nature, but suddenly finds they're alone and sad, Freud would focus on the components of the dream—hiking, nature, alone, and sad.

In free association, his subject would free associate on the symbols and say anything that came to mind, perhaps noting they liked the idea of hiking more than the actual activity and feels sad and alone because they miss a hiking buddy who has recently died.

From that, the hiker might realize they were romanticizing a part of their past—that although they enjoyed the companionship, they didn't really enjoy the activity, but it was something done for a friend. So, perhaps hiking was actually about socializing instead of a love of hiking itself.

Whereas Freudian dream analysis has been disputed or expanded by others who have followed Freud, his ideas served as the jumping-off point for modern dream analysis. They continue to play an important role in understanding the content of what we experience while we sleep.

THE SCIENCE OF DREAMING

The scientific study of dreaming is known as *oneirology*. This area of study doesn't focus so much on the content or meaning of dreams but, rather, the mechanics of dreaming. It looks at the stages of sleep when dreaming occurs as well as how the brain functions during dreams.

REM Sleep

As we touched on at the beginning of this chapter, dreaming occurs during a stage of sleep called rapid eye movement, or REM. This sleep stage was discovered by pioneering sleep researcher Eugene Aserinsky in the

1950s, when during sleep studies he noticed the sleepers' eyes appeared to flutter behind their eyelids while they were in certain sleep stages. Waking subjects during this stage, Aserinsky was able to confirm that, while this was happening, the sleeper was dreaming. He also discovered that brain activity during REM was similar to brain activity when one is awake. He identified several periods of REM throughout a single night of sleep. According to Aserinsky's research, dreams last, on average, five to 20 minutes, and, during dreaming, the release of certain neurotransmitters is repressed so one doesn't act out the content of dreams while asleep. This is why, for example, if you're physically fighting in a dream you don't punch your partner in your sleep.

Dreaming during Other Stages of Sleep

Originally, oneirologists believed dreaming only occurred during REM sleep; however, recent studies have shown dreaming likely occurs in other stages as well. There are three other stages of sleep called NREM (non-REM). When sleepers are awakened during these stages, many are able to recall dreams they were having. Scientists theorize everyone (even people who don't believe they dream) spends an average of six years of their lives dreaming!

Defining Dreams

Oneirologists also have come up with a definition of dreams that has three basic components.

Thinking in the absence of external stimuli. A dream is a form of thinking that occurs when the ego (the "I" or sense of self) shuts down, external stimuli are blocked, and there is a certain level of brain activity (e.g., when you're asleep or unconscious).

We experience dreams through our senses. Dreams are experienced, as opposed to viewed, because they impart sensory data and evoke emotions.

Dreams are what we remember. The dream is what you remember upon waking, so what you notice as a dream is actually a memory of the experience of the dream. And we all automatically apply some form of interpretation to our dreams—the dream is your written or spoken report of the experience of the memory.

Things That Affect Dreams

Various stimuli can affect the type and content of dreams we have. These include the use of drugs and medications, which can cause strange or repressed dreams; melatonin, which can cause extremely vivid dreams; alcohol, which causes fragmented sleep; psychological trauma and conditions such as post-traumatic stress disorder, which can cause vivid replaying of a trauma or representations of that trauma in dreams; and mental illness. Our memories, experiences, and attachments also affect the content of our dreams.

If you've ever tackled a tricky issue by "sleeping on it," you're onto something. Dreams provide a powerful method of problem solving. I often use dreams to assist when I have to make a big decision or when I'm trying to figure out a persistent issue. I state my intention to work on a problem before I go to sleep, and when I wake, I often have a solution or a partial solution I can build upon.

SPIRITUAL ASSOCIATIONS

Over the years, I've discovered that the content of my dreams often leads me to deeper understandings about my path in life. In fact, many dreamers use their dreams as spiritual tools, which can be used to spur spiritual growth and promote greater understanding of oneself as an embodied soul. In my case, it was a dream I had about healing someone by placing my hands on them that encouraged me to explore the healing modality of Reiki and become a certified practitioner.

Mythical Relationships

Dreams often appear in myths and stories as a way to help the dreamer move forward spiritually. Consider that some authors will relay the dreams of characters in novels and stories. Used in this way, the dreams can provide glimpses into the psyche of the characters so readers can better understand their motives. For example, Scrooge's dreams in Dickens's *A Christmas Carol* reveal both his current attitude and how his life could be if he was kinder, and in *War and Peace*, Tolstoy writes of Pierre's terrifying dream of being attacked by dogs, which makes him assess his "evil passions." Dream worlds also often appear as plot devices, such as in Lewis Carroll's *Alice's Adventures in Wonderland,* and in L. Frank Baum's *The Wonderful Wizard of Oz.* In tales such as these, the dreamer awakens having learned a valuable life lesson ("There's no place like home.") and exhibits emotional and spiritual growth. The characters were able to enjoy this growth because they were open to the lessons in their dreams.

Manifesting Prosperity

Dreaming can also help change how you think about certain aspects of your life, such as prosperity. In New Age thought and according to the Law of Attraction (a theory of New Age thought that suggests our thoughts become the things in our lives), when one struggles with prosperity, it is often because we're stuck in a state of "lack consciousness" where beliefs about money keep prosperity from manifesting. Simply stating the intent to have your dreams help you change your thoughts about abundance can help alter your thinking in waking life, allowing you to grow and move forward. A simple statement of intent each night before you go to sleep ("Tonight I will see myself as prosperous in my dreams.") can

help you visualize prosperity while you sleep, which can, in turn, help you visualize prosperity in your waking state.

Finding a New Path

Your dreams often provide information you are unable or unwilling to see when you are awake. This frequently serves as the impetus for spiritual growth. These dreams aren't necessarily divinatory or prophetic in nature but, rather, come as a conduit from your higher self to uncover aspects of yourself that keep you from growing spiritually or to gently nudge you in the direction of spiritual growth.

For example, as I mentioned, I am an intuitive energy healer and Reiki (a form of energy healing) Master-Teacher. I often receive inspiration for my work from my dreams. Recently, I dreamed of a *kanji* (Japanese writing) character I had never seen before. In the dream, I "awoke" from the dream and felt the invisible hands of all the Reiki Masters in the spiritual realm on me and I experienced a brilliant white light swirling with every color imaginable surrounding me and entering my body. I asked the Reiki Masters what it was; they said it was Dragon Reiki that would help me embody the Reiki energy. When I woke, I looked up the symbol I'd seen in my dream and discovered it was the kanji character for "raku." Searching further, I learned there is a form of Reiki called Raku-kei Reiki. I believe my dream was higher guidance telling me that exploring Raku-kei Reiki is the natural next step in my own personal energy healing spiritual journey. I took heed and am currently studying Raku-kei Reiki.

You can use your dreams in the same way. Let them help you process connections you may not understand in your waking life. Give this a try: Before you go to sleep, say to the universe, "Tell me what I need to know to grow." Then, pay attention to the content of your dreams.

Uncovering Shadows

Your dreams can also show you the parts of yourself that lurk in the shadows. Known as shadow work, you can use the content of your dreams to shine a light on the darkest corners of yourself in order to reintegrate those parts of yourself you have disowned.

For example, many people carry unrecognized guilt or shame (shame is guilt that has become stuck and embodied). This unacknowledged guilt can be psychologically and spiritually devastating and can lead to all sorts of unhealthy

unconscious beliefs about oneself. For example, someone abused as a child may have a deep sense of shame about the abuse, believing it was somehow their fault, they deserved it, or they contributed to it. So often, the shame from these traumatic events is buried deep inside, but it can be unconsciously expressed in the ways the person acts, thinks, and feels as an adult.

An adult with unrecognized or unacknowledged shame related to past abuse, for instance, may subconsciously choose partners who continue the abuse because they now believe they deserve it. The power of dreams is that they can help a person uncover this shame, process it, and release it so they can make healthier choices going forward.

An example of this comes from a dream shared with me by a friend who endured abuse as a child. She related that she dreamed of her abusive parent screaming, "I hate you," over and over at her. In the dream, my friend looked at the screaming parent and said, "Well, I forgive you." She tells me that was the day she set down the anger at that parent and refused to allow it to affect her life any longer. This was a powerful way for her to use the content of a dream to spur spiritual growth. The key to doing it is learning to unlock the meaning of your dreams.

COMMON DREAM CONTEXTS

One of the most interesting aspects of dream interpretation is that, although we all dream differently, people often share similar dream contexts. Over the years of teaching classes and writing my column, I've found that many people I encounter have dreams that occur in similar settings or that involve similar types of experiences. These "contexts" are an essential part of dream interpretation. Understanding the settings of your dreams can be key to understanding what a dream is trying to tell you. In the following pages, I share 26 of the most common dream contexts as the first clue to interpreting your dreams. Other aspects of dreams are covered in chapter 2 and will help you further refine the meaning of your dreams beyond context. It's important to note as you work through the process that these contexts may have slightly or completely different meanings based on the dreamer, so, ultimately, the meanings of a dream will vary based on who has dreamed them.

Airport/Airplane

Dreams that take place in an airport or on an airplane are often about higher ideals or lofty goals. They might be telling you a new project is on the horizon, or the dream might be offering a creative solution or idea for a new project. Likewise, it could suggest it's time to start a new venture.

Apocalypse

People are always a little freaked out by apocalyptic dreams—and that's totally understandable. But here's the good news: These dreams aren't nearly as frightening as they seem. Apocalyptic dreams are often about starting over. They may also represent a dramatic shift in perspective, beliefs, or emotional state. Apocalyptic dreams are about the need to destroy a stuck pattern of thought, belief, or behavior in order to be open to something new that will move you in a direction to serve your highest good.

Bathroom

Bathroom dreams are about cleansing and eliminating that which is no longer needed. They may express your unconscious desire for purification as well.

Beach/Ocean/Bodies of Water

Water in dreams is always about emotion, so if you're dreaming of water, you're learning something about your current emotional state. Pay attention to the clarity of the water (are you clear about your emotions or are they "muddy"?) as well as the state of the water. Smooth water indicates peaceful emotions, whereas rough water represents more tumultuous feelings.

Boat

Dreams that take place on a boat are about navigating your emotions. As with other dreams based on water, pay attention to the water clarity and conditions. Notice how the boat moves through the different types of water. Is the boat smoothly cutting through big waves? This indicates you are handling your tumultuous emotions well. However, if the boat is being tossed about on choppy seas, it suggests you feel emotional disequilibrium. If a boat is being tossed about on smooth water, it may suggest you are overreacting to something.

Cellar/Underground/Dark Place

Dreams that occur in cellars, underground, or are just overall very dark in ambience are about your shadow-self, or that part of yourself you want to keep hidden because you have disowned it. These dreams urge you to shine a light on your shadows so they no longer control your life.

Cemetery

Perhaps not surprisingly, cemetery dreams are about unresolved grief and sadness. Interestingly, although we most traditionally relate grief to death of a loved one, it can be about anything you are grieving, such as the loss of a job or relationship, a child growing up and leaving the nest, or even a passage from one stage of your life to another.

Church/Spiritual Place

When any place you consider highly spiritual shows up in a dream, this is a sign the dream has spiritual guidance to offer. These places may also suggest the dream is talking about something sacred to you.

Courtroom/Courthouse

Dreams that take place in these locations are about judgment. They may suggest you feel judged, or are judging yourself or another unfairly or unkindly.

Daytime/Nighttime

You can learn a lot about your dream from the time of day in which it takes place. Daytime and nighttime are opposites on a spectrum of duality found in the Taoist concept of yin and yang. Daytime is yang. In dreams, it can represent active energy, masculinity, cheerfulness, aggression, ambition, hardness, or drive. Nighttime is yin, and represents feminine energy that is mysterious, dark, yielding, flowing, and passive. Daytime represents light and consciousness whereas nighttime represents shadows and subconscious. Neither is inherently better or worse than the other; both flow one into the other along the spectrum of day to night and both are necessary in the cycle of life.

Sometimes, you'll dream it's light during the night and dark during the day. This can remind you that no matter where you are the other element is always present. If you dream it's light at night, for instance, it may remind you that even during darker times, there is always light.

Dreams About Dreaming

Dreams within a dream often suggest you are not paying attention to a very real situation in your life. This could be because you don't believe it is important, or you are in denial. Pay careful attention to dreams that appear within a dream. That dream can guide you to something you need to give more attention or notice to.

Elevator

The elevator is a vehicle of movement and these dreams are about aspiration and the direction you are moving in your life. Pay attention to the way the elevator moves, whether it lets you off on the floor you desire, if you're stuck, etc. All scenarios speak to how you feel about your life's direction.

Forest/Woods

Dreams that occur in the forest are about navigating the unknown or things we believe are mysterious about ourselves. You can better understand the meaning of the forest in a dream by looking at how woods are often depicted in fairy tales, which often provide the mythology of youth. In these stories, the forest is often a mysterious, dark, slightly scary place the hero has to navigate to achieve a goal.

Funeral

Funeral dreams are about endings, just as funerals in waking life are about endings. These dreams allow you to acknowledge and grieve the ending of something important, or they may be telling you it is time to bring something to an end that no longer serves you.

Garden/Nature

Dreams about nature are typically about spiritual renewal. This is especially true if you are someone who goes out into nature for spiritual fulfillment or to be uplifted. Dreams set in gardens are about abundance and prosperity. Notice the state of the garden. Is it withered? If so, chances are you need to work on your beliefs about abundance. If the garden is verdant and lush, it suggests your abundance consciousness is working for you. If the garden is just blooming, it suggests that steps you are taking to improve abundance are beginning to pay off.

Hospital/Health Care Facility

These dreams are about health and healing. Usually this is physical healing, but it can also be spiritual or emotional healing. It may suggest you need to pay attention to your physical health, or it might suggest now is the time to work on healing spiritual or emotional issues.

Hotel

Dreams that take place in hotels are about transitions. A hotel is a temporary place and, when you dream of them, they remind you that things are often temporary. A hotel-based dream can also suggest you are in a transitional state in your life.

House/Mansion

Dreams are ultimately very self-involved because they give us messages about ourselves. Dreams featuring a house or a mansion are about you—you are the house—and the many rooms are various aspects of your personality. The state of the house is important. Is it chaotic? Empty? Overstuffed? In disrepair? These all offer clues as to how you are feeling about yourself emotionally, spiritually, mentally, or physically.

Jail/Prison

Dreams that occur in prison or jail may suggest you feel trapped or stuck. They also may suggest you feel guilty about something, believe you are being punished, or think you should be punished.

School

Schools of all kinds are probably the most common dream context. Virtually everyone has regular dreams about school and many people have similar recurring dreams about school. Most people can recall a dream in which they haven't been to class, have a big test but haven't studied, and the like. Perhaps, not surprisingly, school dreams are about learning, lessons, and personal growth. These dreams often offer clues about how you can learn, grow, and change, or the ways you are avoiding doing so.

Sex

Although sex dreams can actually be about the desire for sex, more frequently the dreams are about the desire to establish intimacy with yourself or another, or to make more intimate connections in your life.

Store

Dreams taking place in stores or where you shop are about making choices in life. It may also mean you have a desire for something new in your life.

Underwater

Dreaming that you are underwater is about being immersed in emotion. Notice how you feel. Do you feel safe? Are you breathing freely? If yes, this indicates you feel comfortable in spite of powerful emotions. If you are panicked, being chased, or feel afraid or uncomfortable, chances are you feel overwhelmed by your emotions instead.

Vehicle/Car/Truck

Dreams that occur in a vehicle, such as a car or truck, are about your path in life. Notice, in these dreams, who is driving. Is someone else driving? This may mean you feel you are currently allowing someone else to control your path. If you're driving, how's it going? Do your brakes work? Do you feel in control or out of control? The answers to these questions offer clues to how you feel about your path. For example, if your brakes fail or you're crashing into things, you may feel like you don't have a lot of control of your life path right now.

Work

Work dreams are often about your career path, but they can be about anything you are "working at" right now. So, if you are working on emotional healing, for instance, you may have a work dream. Notice things such as how you feel. Are you overwhelmed? Is the work easy or difficult? Are you enjoying it or resenting it? These characteristics offer clues to how you feel about the work you are doing.

Common Contexts, Uncommon Experiences

Although there are many common contexts, remember these are general. Whereas these are likely explanations of what your dream is about, these contexts may have personal meanings to you that are different from the common meanings, so it's always important to look at personal beliefs and experiences before you default to a collective one.

THE HISTORY OF DREAMS IS THE HISTORY OF YOU

As we have discussed in this chapter, ideas about dreams and their meanings have changed and shifted throughout history. Different experts have varying theories about what dreams mean and how they can be interpreted. And although some theories have fallen out of fashion, understanding the history of dream interpretation, the various methods of understanding dream types and symbols, and the context in which dreams occur all come together to create a framework for interpreting your dreams and decoding what they say about your unconscious feelings, understandings, and drives.

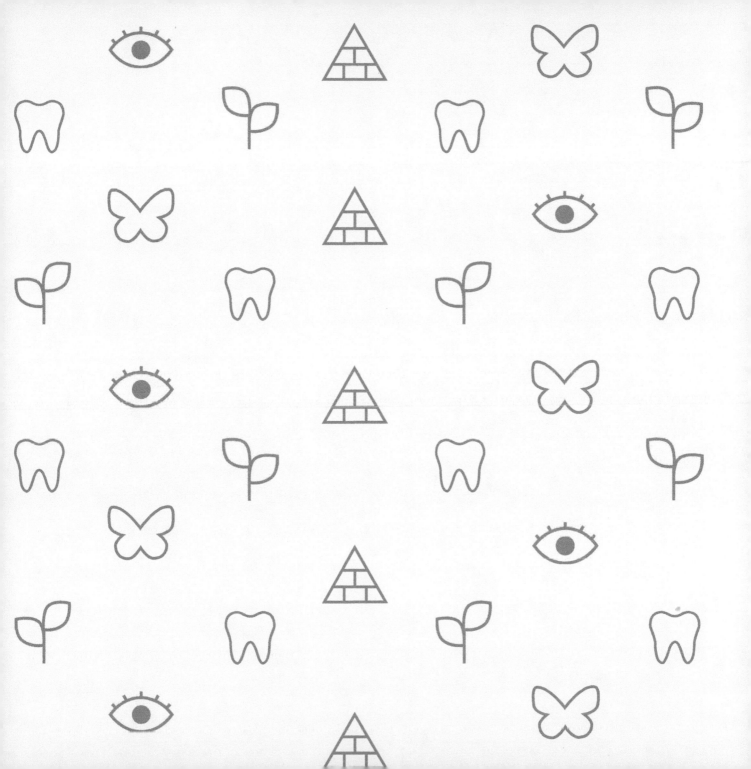

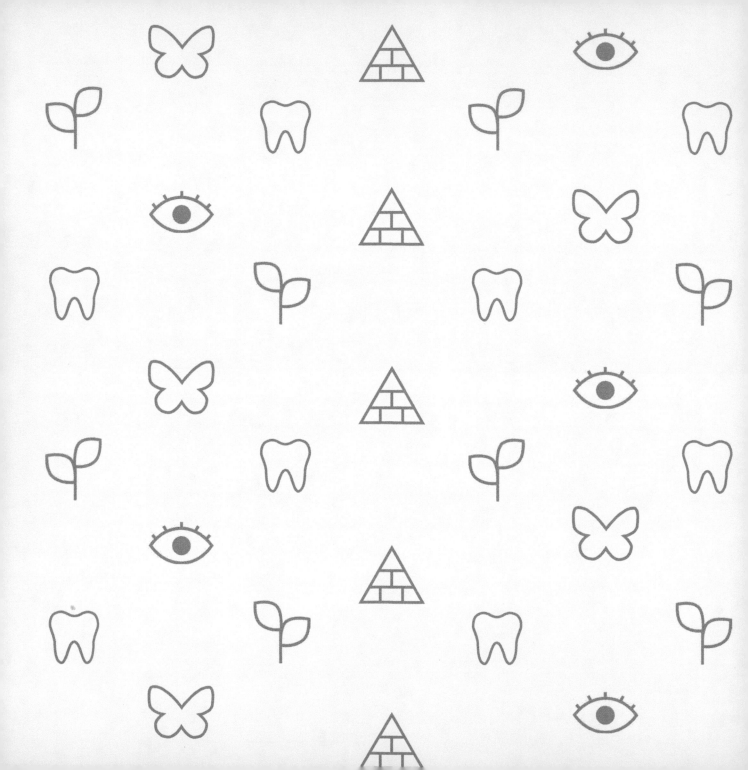

CHAPTER TWO

VARIATIONS, ARCHETYPES, AND SYMBOLS

We all have more than one type of dream. Some dreams are highly symbolic and require interpretation, whereas others are more mundane and not worth the time to translate. In this chapter, we'll delve into which types of dreams are significant and how to recognize them. Before you can begin interpretation, you'll also need to understand common dream tropes as well as the archetypes and people that appear in your dreams, so you can weave them into the interpretive process. You'll learn about all that in this chapter.

VARIATIONS ON A DREAM

Some dreams are significant and others less so. Knowing which is which can save you a lot of time in dream interpretation. Fortunately, there are several common types of dreams as well as common characteristics that make interpretation-worthy dreams easier to recognize. Even though everyone dreams differently, most people have similar types of dreams.

Daily Processing Dreams

These types of dreams are a form of brain maintenance, where your brain sorts memories from the day for long-term storage. When you have these types of dreams, they don't seem terribly significant and they are the type of dream you are most likely to forget because their content is mundane. If, in your dream, you're going about activities similar to what you do in your waking life, such as going to work, following routines, or doing chores, chances are it is a processing and memory-sorting dream. These dreams appear factual and easy to follow and understand. These dreams might also include reactions to the physical environment while you sleep. For instance, you might notice you're hot or cold in the dream, or you may notice your ankle hurts in the dream if you twisted it that day.

Psychological Processing Dreams

These dreams are significant because they reveal things about your psyche that you may not be aware of while awake. Psychological processing dreams can reveal anxiety and fears, for example. They can also reveal hopes or ambitions (similar to Freud's idea of wish fulfillment), or they may help you work through problems. These dreams are symbolic and often don't make a lot of chronological sense, but when you start to look at the symbols, you can uncover subconscious psychological issues. For example, I used to have a dream in which I got into an elevator and, no matter what I did, the elevator wouldn't stop at my floor. I realized that the dream was showing my frustration with my career and represented me feeling as if my career was out of my control. Like the elevator in my dream, my career was leading me instead of me controlling my career. Believe it or not—when I changed careers, the dreams stopped.

Recurring Dreams

Everyone has recurring dreams, although they may shift and change over one's lifetime. You may find that a recurring dream is exactly the same every time, or it may have recurring elements or a familiar sense or feel from dream to dream but be slightly different in content. The most important thing to realize is that these dreams reveal ongoing issues we have in our lives that we aren't addressing or coping with well. For example, when I was in my early twenties, I had a recurring dream I was in a car that was rolling downhill toward a lake and my brakes and steering didn't work. The dream was there to show me I felt my life was out of control—which, at the time, it was. The meaning of specific recurring dreams can change over your lifetime, so each time you have the dream it's important to evaluate it within the context of what is happening in your life at that time.

Nightmares

Although nightmares can feel terrifying and disconcerting, they actually serve a valuable purpose. Nightmares have a much stronger emotional impact than most other dreams, so they often contain the strongest messages for us about things we need to recognize but are failing to. For instance, a nightmare about being chased by a UFO could suggest you feel alienated in some aspect of your life and it is causing significant psychological distress.

Prophetic Dreams

Inevitably when I teach dream workshops, someone asks me how to have prophetic dreams, which are dreams that show you snippets of something coming in the near future. Their content may be symbolic or literal.

For example, I dream of events such as earthquakes before they occur. Normally if I have an earthquake dream, an earthquake occurs within 48 hours of the dream somewhere in the world. For example, in October 1989 I was visiting San Francisco the day before the Loma Prieta earthquake. The night before, I dreamed of Earth shaking and, when I woke, I told my husband we needed to leave because an earthquake was coming. We left that morning, missing the earthquake by a matter of hours.

I spent a lot of time worrying about my prophetic dreams once I recognized the pattern, because I realized I knew something was going to happen but I couldn't do a thing about it since I had no specific information. I started using the content of those dreams to do the only thing I could—send love and healing energy to the situation.

It may take time to sort out whether you're having prophetic dreams. You usually realize it after the fact when the thing you dreamed about occurs. Keeping a dream journal can help you recognize patterns in dreaming that may indicate prophetic dreams.

Lucid Dreams

Lucid dreams can be fun because you control the content of the dream while you're asleep, making these a bit like a choose-your-own-adventure game. How do you know if you're having a lucid dream? If, in the dream, you can control the direction it takes, you are lucid dreaming. This comes naturally to some people, but others can learn it with practice. Although lucid dreaming is beyond the scope of this book, one way to learn lucid dreaming is to state your intent to have a lucid dream each night before you go to sleep. If it doesn't work at first, keep at it. Sometimes it takes some time for this to occur, but with practice you can turn any dream into a lucid one if you wish.

Inspirational Dreams

Dreams of inspiration offer guidance for creative problem solving. These are the dreams we're thinking of when we talk about an artist having a "light bulb moment" or a creative breakthrough. I experience this often. I will go to sleep thinking about a book, article, or blog post I'd like to write, and I wake with it fully written in my head. These dreams are vivid and frequently symbolic, so they often don't make a lot of sense until you interpret them. However, you can recognize these dreams because they seem vivid and memorable and often are accompanied by a sense of hope, inspiration, or joy.

On Daydreaming

I've always been a big daydreamer, especially when I was younger. For me, daydreaming is a form of visualization, helping me set things I'd like to accomplish more deeply in my psyche. I also find it's a great source of creative problem solving.

But what does science say about daydreaming? Is it a big waste of time, or does it serve some greater purpose?

The fact is, daydreaming can be quite productive. According to a study published in *Creativity Research Journal*, children who daydream are more creative. Daydreaming offers them a way to explore interests and engage in creative pursuits.

Allowing your mind to wander into daydreams is similar to going into a trancelike state. When you're there, similar to entering hypnosis, your mind is more susceptible to suggestion. Therefore, if you choose to allow your daydreams to wander in a positive direction, you can reap real benefits including:

★ A much-needed break for your brain
★ Creative problem solving
★ Formation of new neural connections
★ Memory consolidation and storage
★ Visualization of goals and aspirations

Daydreaming is a great tool for working with the Law of Attraction as well. Because you are awake, you can consciously control the content of your daydreams, choosing positive emotional visualizations that allow you to see yourself achieving your goals. When you do this, you create a neurological link that can help you think more positively and take proactive steps to reach those goals.

Visitation Dreams

Psychic mediums and others who communicate with spirits suggest the easiest way for a spirit to communicate with people is in a dream state while their mind is, effectively, shut off. The hallmarks of visitation dreams are that they often have a hyperreal quality to them and, in the dream, you're talking to someone who is no longer alive. You often wake from these dreams feeling as if you've had a visit from a lost loved one. I truly believe these dreams are a real form of communication from the other side.

So, go ahead and daydream. It is especially beneficial if you're feeling mental fatigue. Take five minutes, sit back, and let your mind wander.

WHO'S IN YOUR DREAMS—JUNGIAN ARCHETYPES AND OTHER PEOPLE

Our dreams tend to be very self-centered; they are almost always about us. So, when we dream of other people, those people represent aspects of ourselves our subconscious wants us to pay attention to. Occasionally people in dreams represent someone else, but in general they tend to be highly symbolic of aspects of ourselves. For example, if you dream of someone who has darker hair, darker eyes, a darker skin tone, or darker clothing than you typically wear, these people are often a representation of your shadow, or that part of yourself you dislike and wish to keep hidden.

Dreams where people have a lot of importance can also represent archetypes. According to Carl Jung, archetypes are representations of certain overarching themes or types of people with universal characteristics, such as being a nurturer or a rescuer.

Dream People and Personal Symbolism

When trying to decipher meaning, I always suggest you look to personal symbolism before you consider archetypes, which arise from the collective consciousness. When another person appears in your dreams, ask yourself the following:

★ What does that person mean to me?
★ How do I feel when I see or think about that person?

- ★ How do I identify that person in my life?
- ★ What parts of me do I see reflected in that person?
- ★ What is that person's role in my life?
- ★ If I could describe that person in one or two words, what would they be?

Jungian Archetypes

Jung believed certain representations of people that resided in the collective unconscious were universal types of characters. He listed several archetypes, which may appear as people in your dreams. If someone in your dreams fits any of the common archetypes that follow and they don't fit within your personal symbolism, then they may represent an archetypal energy.

When working with archetypes, it's important to understand they were developed during a very different time. Thus, many archetypes are extremely Eurocentric in their descriptions and presentations. It's always important to keep cultural considerations in mind with archetypes and realize that people from different cultures and backgrounds may experience archetypal energies in ways that reflect their own cultural upbringing.

Persona. The identity you project to others is persona. Virtually everyone is different privately than publicly and, to some extent, we all wear a social mask. Your social mask is the persona archetype. When you appear as a character in your dreams, this is the persona appearing. You may recognize a character in your dreams as you, even if the character doesn't resemble you physically. For example, if you dream you are a cat, even though you are most clearly not a cat in real life, the dream is showing you that part of the mask you wear has some type of cat energy (such as being super independent).

Shadow. I find that dreams are often about our shadow selves. Jung identified this archetype as the parts of yourself you may be ashamed of, repress, keep hidden, or have disowned in some way. This may include negative emotions or traits you have disowned. This archetype can appear in dreams in many ways. They can literally be a shadow, for instance, or the shadow can also be embodied in a person appearing in your dreams. For example, it may be someone with darker hair, eyes, or skin than yours, or it may be a shadowy figure, such as a thief or a murderer. The shadow's appearance often leaves you feeling uneasy and they frequently appear in nightmares. Shadows in dreams encourage you to confront issues about yourself you don't want to see.

Anima/Animus. The anima/animus represents the female and male aspects of your personality, or the polarity of traits such as yin and yang or female and male. Everyone is a balance of energies; nobody is 100 percent one or the other, and balance between opposites serves a valuable purpose. In your dream, the anima or animus will be either a very masculine (animus) character, or very feminine (anima). Alternately, these archetypes may have some exaggerated masculine or feminine aspect or show a balance of both.

Animus and anima may also show up with a very specific "feel" to them; you notice their energy feels excessively masculine or feminine, for instance. When the anima or animus appears in your dreams, they remind you to create balance and integration between opposite aspects of your character.

Divine Child/Innocent. This sweet child represents your purest self—that divine part of you that is innocent and true. Often, this manifests as a blond, blue-eyed cherub, but any child appearing in your dreams, especially a baby, may be a representation of the Divine Child. When it appears in dreams, the Divine Child reminds you to hold on to your true self and maintain and nurture the purest part of you. Alternately, it could suggest you are being too trusting.

Wise One. Often appearing as a wise old man or woman, this is the archetype of the sage or mentor in dreams. These may be represented as an authority figure, such as a teacher, spiritual leader, guru, or mentor. When the wise one appears in dreams, pay attention. These are dreams of guidance. If you ascribe to any faith, Jesus, Buddha, and other religious figures may show up as the wise one, as might angels or guides.

Trickster. The trickster archetype is often responsible for our strangest dreams. It may show up as something such as a jester or comedian, or it may be a character that suddenly changes its attributes partway through the dream. Tricksters in dreams come to remind you to lighten up, or may be pointing out some error in judgment you've made that could lead to embarrassment if you don't correct it.

Great Mother. The Great Mother is a nurturer, often a maternal figure such as a mom, a grandmother, an aunt, or someone with mom energy. When she shows up in your dreams, the Great Mother reminds you to nurture yourself deeply. She also may show up in dreams to provide reassurance.

Hero. In our dreams, we are all equally the hero and the scapegoat. The hero archetype is a common one; it appears in virtually every book of fiction ever written. In dreams, the hero is often someone who saves the day. The hero may also arrive in the form of someone you respect deeply, such as a boss, mentor, or coach, or it may actually be a classic hero, such as a superhero or a warrior. When the hero appears in dreams, it represents confidence and bravery, showing you ways you can resolve issues and move forward with conviction.

Fool. The fool is similar to the innocent; it's a well-known archetype. In fact, in the tarot deck, The Fool is the first card of the major arcana, a grouping of archetypal cards that represent the journey from innocence through a dark night of the soul and all the way to enlightenment. The fool may show up as a hapless wanderer or someone who seems spacey or very present focused. He wanders through life, focused on his adventure in the present moment. The fool reminds you to take life as it comes and stay focused on the moment at hand instead of worrying about the future or living in the past.

Magician. The Magician is another archetype in a tarot deck's major arcana. He is an alchemist, somebody who can bring creations to life. Often, the magician in dreams is a shape-shifter or some type of creative or magical creator (or it can literally be a magician). When appearing in your dreams, the magician is there to remind you that you have all the tools needed to turn your dreams into a reality.

Hermit. This is another archetype that also appears in the major arcana. In dreams, the hermit may appear as a loner or someone who spends time away from others. When the hermit appears in your dreams, it's a reminder to spend time alone in meditation, contemplation, or spiritual learning.

When we dream of other people, those people represent aspects of ourselves that our subconscious wants us to pay attention to.

NUMBERS AND COLORS IN DREAMS

It's not just people and symbols in dreams that are significant. Numbers, colors, shapes, and even things like items of clothing can provide more information about your dream's meaning. These serve as modifiers to help you better understand what your dream is trying to tell you.

Numbers and colors can appear in many ways. Note as many details as you can about your dreams. For example, three of something may be significant, or if you notice someone is wearing a certain color shirt, that could be meaningful. If a number or color stands out to you, it's probably important. Interestingly, numbers are almost always considered as single digits except in the case of three numbers that are considered master numbers, 11, 22, and 33. So, if you see the number 14 in your dream, it either represents the digits 1 and 4 or the reduction of the digits (adding them together), so in this case, 5. The numbers 11, 22, and 33 each have their own meaning. Here are some ways numbers and colors might appear in dreams:

★ A number may appear on a door, a telephone, etc.
★ Someone may say a number.
★ You may notice a date circled on a calendar.
★ You may see a certain number of objects, such as three balls, a set of twins (two), four apples in a bowl, six chairs around a table, etc.
★ Colors can appear as colors of vehicles, clothing, décor, etc.

★ Any color that stands out is significant. For example, I once had a dream I was hitting various colors of golf balls onto a driving range. The colors of the balls stood out and, when I interpreted my dreams, they were all significant for what was happening in my life.

SHAPES

Sometimes a shape will stand out in your dreams. Granted, everything has a shape, but if you notice a particular shape, then, like a color or a number, it can have meaning that modifies the main content of your dream. For example, if you specifically notice a round table or you dream of spheres or pyramids, these may be significant. Shape may appear in the following ways:

★ You may see art with a shape on it.
★ You may notice something has an unusual shape, such as a triangular table.
★ Shapes may appear in logos, on clothing, etc.
★ Someone may speak the word of a shape to you.

Shapes have meaning in sacred geometry as well. Certain shapes have symbolic meanings. You may also notice shapes as things such as characters. For example, sometimes I see astrological symbols in my dreams representing either a specific astrological sign or a planet. By looking into the meanings of those symbols, I can interpret what it is telling me in my dream.

Detailing a Dream

In my classes and column, I've discovered many people have a variation of the recurring dream Steven details here. Recurring dreams often take place because there's something in your life, or some aspect of yourself, that remains unacknowledged and needs notice, care, and integration. I have a version of this dream a few times a year, usually when I feel overwhelmed. Once, I was discussing dreams with my dad and my son and I discovered they both have had a version of the same dream. This phenomenon is so common that when I bring this dream up in classes I teach, almost everyone in the class nods their heads in recognition. I've also had people write to me with various versions of the dream for interpretation in my column. Here is one person's version of the dream and what it means. If you have a similar dream, your dream's meaning is probably along the same lines.

Steven's Dream

I have a recurring dream in which I am in high school. It is finals week of my senior year and I need to pass all of my classes to graduate. However, I haven't been to my classes and, in fact, I don't even know where my classrooms are. I haven't cracked a book and I haven't studied. I'm in a panic knowing I'm going to tank my finals and not be able to graduate with the rest of my class.

Interpretation

Sound familiar? This is a common anxiety dream usually about work (although if you're still in school, it could be about school). The dream typically means you're afraid you aren't doing well at work, that you may be failing, or that you are afraid of being fired. It also may reflect a general lack of confidence in your job or studies.

Here are the meanings of different shapes that might appear in your dreams:

Circles represent protection, influence, completion, balance, regeneration, or unity. They can also represent cycles.

Spirals represent the unfolding of spirituality or walking one's path in life.

Triangles may represent religion, or they may have the same meanings as the number three (see page 44). They can also represent success or reaching the pinnacle of something.

Squares and rectangles may have the same meanings as the number four (see page 44), or they may represent stability or materialism. They also represent dependability, safety, and shelter.

Crosses frequently represent Christianity, but they can also represent things that come in fours, like the elements.

Pentagrams may represent manifestation, femininity, Earth, or the Wicca religion.

Vesica piscis (two circles side by side, overlapping) represent illumination, enlightenment, or divinity.

Infinity symbol represents, not surprisingly, infinity.

Pyramids symbolize integration of body, mind, and spirit.

Spheres represent the universe and nonduality (that is, the inclusion of all in the one).

NUMBER	MEANING
1	Autonomy * Ego * Getting back to basics * Independence * Individuality * Leadership * Loneliness * Originality * Pioneering spirit * Rebellion * Selfishness * Self-reliance * Simplicity * Singularity * Stubbornness * Unlimited potential * Weakness
2	Balance of opposites * Carelessness * Duality * Femininity * Humility * Intuition * Oversensitivity * Partnership * Patience * Qualities that come in twos or pairs, such as happy/sad * Resilience * Yin/yang
3	Creativity * Extravagance * Exuberance * Hypocrisy * Imagination * Impatience * Inner strength * Intolerance or prejudice * Joy * Optimism * Overindulgence * Self-exploration * Self-expression * Spirituality * Talent * Vitality
4	Conscientiousness * Hard work * Honesty * Lack of imagination * Limitation * Methodical * Reliability * Stability * Stubborn * Trustworthiness
5	Adaptability * Adventure * Boldness * Carelessness * Curiosity * Daring * Irresponsibility * Sociability * Spontaneity * Taking action * Versatility * Wit
6	Anxiety * Balance * Bliss * Community * Compassion * Cooperation * Cynicism * Idealism * Jealousy * Loyalty * Nature * Perfection * Protection * Suspicion * Union

NUMBER	MEANING
7	Connection to higher power ★ Divinity ★ Healing ★ Intelligence ★ Lack of trustworthiness ★ Luck ★ Perseverance ★ Sarcasm ★ Social awkwardness ★ Spirituality ★ Wisdom
8	Control ★ Greed ★ Infinite ★ Insensitivity ★ Intuition ★ Karma ★ Power ★ Success ★ Violence
9	Arrogance ★ Closure ★ Compassion ★ Completion ★ Creativity ★ Egocentricity ★ Fickleness ★ Generosity ★ Inspiration ★ Rebirth ★ Self-sufficiency
11	Anxiety ★ Charisma ★ Innate wisdom ★ Instinct ★ Intuition ★ Lack of focus ★ Stress
22	Ambition ★ Balance ★ Discipline ★ Manifestation ★ Pragmatism ★ Precision
33	Ascension ★ Humanitarianism ★ Knowledge ★ Mastery ★ Understanding ★ Unnecessary piety
2-digit #s	Other two-digit numbers must be reduced. Add the numbers together to get the reduced number or translate each number separately based on the meaning for the single digit.
0	Zero appears rarely unless it's as a written or spoken number. Then it means the following: Divinity ★ Emptiness ★ Nothingness ★ Placeholder ★ Space ★ The universe ★ Totality ★ Yin/yang

COLOR	MEANING
White	Angelic realms * Divinity * Higher power * Innocence * New beginnings * Peace * Perfection * Purity
Black	Death * First chakra * Grounding * Hard feelings * Hate * Hidden potential * Hidden qualities * Mourning * Shadow-self * Unconscious * Unknown
Brown	Comfort * Earthiness * Element of wood * Happy home * Nature * Practicality * Worldliness
Gold	Cheerfulness * Determination * Materialism * Prosperity * Self-esteem * Self-worth * Spiritual reward
Silver	Justice * Protection * Purity
Red	Aggression * Anger * Blood * Courage * Energy * Fire * Groundedness * Passion * Vitality * Vigor
Orange	Friendliness * Liveliness * New interests * Place in groups, such as family or society * Sacral chakra * Self-control * Sociability
Yellow	Betrayal * Deceit * Energy * Illness * Intellect * Self-confidence * Solar plexus chakra

COLOR	MEANING
Green	Compassion ★ Fertility ★ Financial reward ★ Growth ★ Healing ★ Jealousy ★ Money ★ Nature ★ Positive changes ★ Romantic love ★ Unconditional love ★ Wealth
Blue	Calmness or tranquility ★ Communication ★ Heaven ★ Honesty ★ Loyalty ★ Open-mindedness ★ Sadness ★ Speaking your truth ★ Throat chakra ★ Truth ★ Wisdom
Purple or Violet	Compassion ★ Deceit ★ Devotion ★ Divinity ★ Healing ★ Insight ★ Justice ★ Protection ★ Psychic ability ★ Royalty ★ Spiritual insight ★ Spirituality ★ Third eye chakra ★ Wealth
Pink	Affection ★ Commitment ★ Compassion ★ Happiness ★ Immaturity ★ Joy ★ Kindness ★ Romantic love ★ Unconditional love
Darker hues	Colors mixed with black that are darker or muddier shades tend to point toward the negative aspects of the color.
Lighter hues	Colors mixed with white for lighter hues or shades tend to point toward the positive aspects of the color.

The Hidden Messages in Dreams

In the early 1950s behavioral psychologist Calvin S. Hall, Jr. formed his own theory of dreams. As with Freud and Jung, he developed his theories before sleep was well studied or understood by science, so no one had yet identified REM sleep as the state where dreams were most likely to occur.

Hall disagreed with Freudian dream interpretation and sought to develop his own theories about the content of dreams. He saw dreams as a cognitive process providing insight into the unconscious mind. When he wrote about his theories in his book *The Meaning of Dreams*, Hall stated images in dreams were the embodiment of thoughts from the waking mind. In other words, dreams are representations of how we view our own lives.

Hall believed you could interpret dreams based on an empirical quantitative coding system he created from analysis of thousands of recorded dreams. According to Hall, in order to interpret dreams, one must know the actions of the dreamer in the dream, the objects in the dream, the dreamer's interaction with others, and the dream's setting. Knowing these things will help you understand the dreamer, not the dream.

According to Hall, dreams could reveal the following about the cognitive processes of the dreamer:

Concepts of self. The roles we play in life and how we see ourselves

Concepts of others. How we see the roles others play in life and how we respond to them

Concepts of conflict. How we see the struggles and issues in our daily life and how we might resolve them

Concepts of the world. How we view the world in which we live, whether we feel safe or unsafe, nurtured or neglected

Concepts of prohibitions, punishment, and impulses. How we view society and its role in our life, whether we fear punishment, or see society as just

Hall felt all these concepts appear regularly in dreams and offered a sort of road map to how we behave, the choices we make, and how we arrive at certain places or situations in our life.

In the 1960s Hall worked with fellow psychologist Robert L. Van de Castle to develop a coding system that allowed for quantitative analysis of dreams based on 16 different scales including characters, social interactions, activities, emotions, settings, objects, and more. Once all these were tracked, a numerical analysis was performed and compared to findings from groups of other dreamers to arrive at a better understanding of the dreamer.

It is important to note Hall's theory of dream interpretation was strictly cognitive. It didn't draw on anything such as symbolism, free association, or similar things. Rather, the interpretation was based entirely on the content of the dream.

Hall's work provided an entirely new way to look at dreams and offered a way for researchers and psychologists to quantify dream content to arrive at a better understanding of the dreamer. As with Freud, Jung, and others, Hall's theories offer insight into dreams and put forth a framework to understand them, allowing us to take a deeper dive into the meaningful content of our dreams.

MANY LAYERS OF MEANING

Interpreting dreams is a fascinating pursuit. Although everyone's mind works a little differently, research has shown there are commonalities among dreamers that allow us to peek inside our subconscious minds. We all have our own personal symbolism that comes from our individual culture, personal experiences, family experiences, religious beliefs, regional beliefs, social circles, and more, and those concepts arise frequently in our dreams as symbols. However, as members of humanity, we also have access to symbols arising from the collective consciousness that have the same meaning across all cultures and belief systems. After examining our dreams for personal symbolism, we can then turn to ideas that are in the collective consciousness, giving us new layers of meanings for a better under-standing of ourselves.

Our subconscious has a great deal to tell us if we understand how it speaks to us: everything from the types of dreams we have to the people, shapes, colors, and numbers in them that help us better understand our unconscious beliefs and motivations, making us aware of things about ourselves we are unable or unwilling to see in our waking lives.

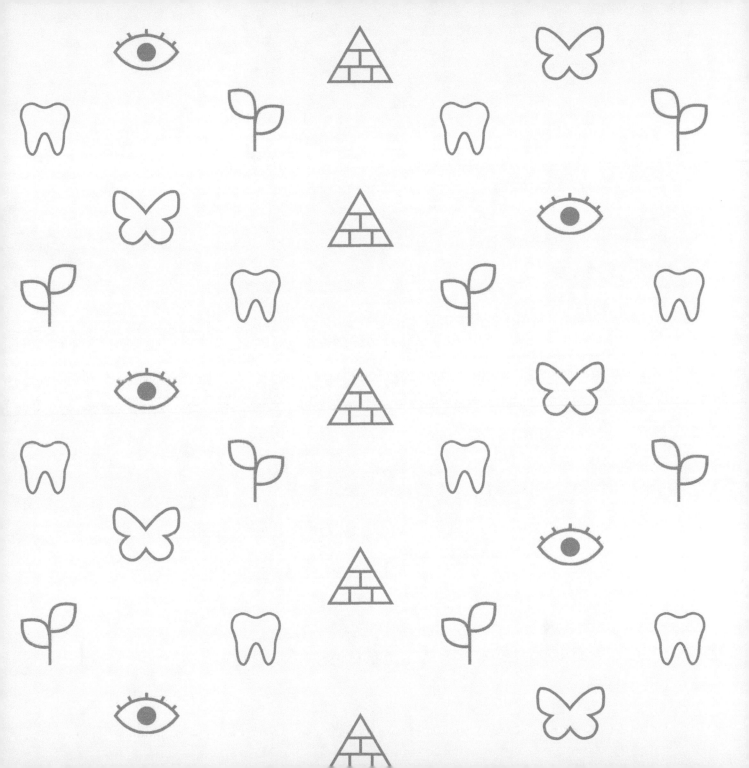

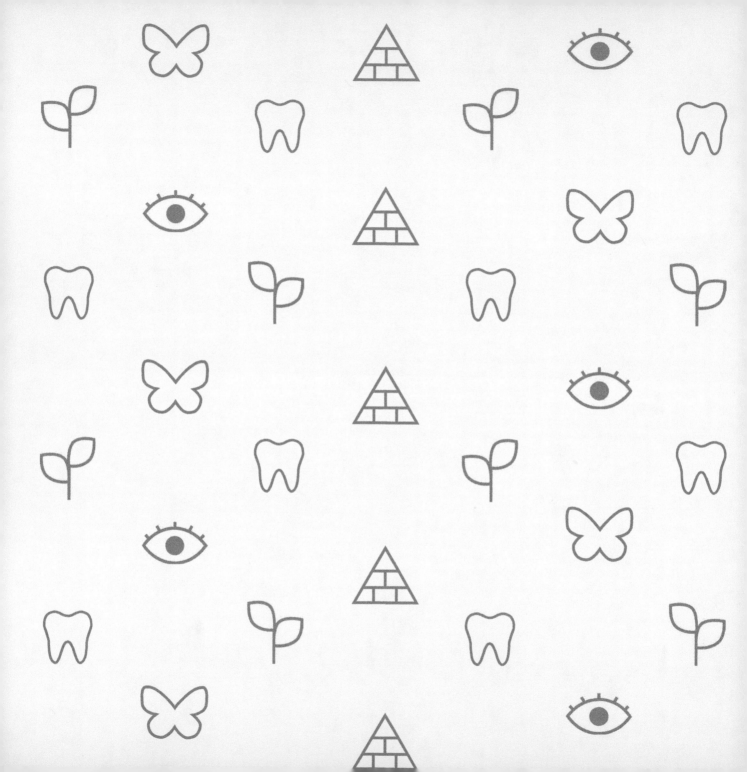

CHAPTER THREE

THE INTERPRETIVE PROCESS

Now that you have some background into dreaming, you're ready to start interpreting your dreams. I'll walk you through the process and provide examples along the way. It's important that before you take a deep dive into interpretation you ask yourself, "What do I think this dream means?" If an answer comes to you, chances are you're right.

As you work through this chapter, keep in mind a dream you've had that you've wondered about. Write down what you think it was about or what it was trying to tell you. Then, apply the steps in the process to the dream to see how close you were. It's important to understand there is no right or wrong answer; the dream interpretation process is a way to access your subconscious and higher guidance, so if something feels right to you, there's a good chance it is.

It's helpful to have a dream journal to record your dreams and interpretations. It doesn't have to be anything official. I just write a word or two on a notepad near my bed if I wake in the middle of the night. In the morning, I record everything I can remember from my dreams in a document on my computer. I use the same document to analyze when I'm working on the interpretation. With that in place, let's get started!

SET INTENTIONS, RELEASE EXPECTATIONS

I have many people tell me that although they remember that they dream, they don't remember the content of their dreams. And if they do recall the content, they feel the information they receive is nonsense or has nothing of value. These are valid concerns; however, I've found through my work with dreamers that with focused intention you can remember dreams and have dreams that impart significant information.

Setting Intentions

An intention is an aim or plan. It sounds simple and possibly not terribly meaningful, but I believe intention is everything. Having a clear intention is the most important thing you can do in any kind of internal or spiritual work, whether it's dream interpretation or something else, such as attracting things you want into your life or creating healing. Your intentions are your lodestar. They light the way so you can guide yourself to what you wish to attain.

An intention isn't exactly a goal. It's a statement of where you're headed. I mentioned earlier that before I go to sleep each night I say, "Tell me what I need to know." This is my statement of intention to my subconscious, to my divine guidance system, and to myself that the content of my dreams will provide the information I need to better understand myself, my spiritual path, or some aspect of my life. It's a simple way to state an intention and you're welcome to use it. You're also welcome to create your personalized statement of intention, such as "Tonight my dreams will contain valuable information that serves my greatest good and, when I wake, I will remember the content of my dreams."

Although your intention can be stated more specifically than that, if you wish, I find a general statement of intention focused on receiving information to serve your highest and greatest good works best. Be consistent in your intention; make sure it's part of your regular pre-sleep ritual. It may take time before your dreams grow more significant, but with your stated intention they will. Just give your subconscious a few nights or weeks to get the message.

Sleep Paralysis and Dreams

Research shows that during REM sleep, chemicals in the brain temporarily relax and inhibit your voluntary muscle movement. Translation: Neurotransmitters temporarily turn off your skeletal muscles during REM sleep. Even though your eyes are rapidly moving in REM, the rest of you isn't. This probably occurs to keep you from acting out your dreams in your sleep so you don't injure yourself or others, particularly during vivid, active dreams.

Sometimes when you wake from this cycle, the brain hasn't yet signaled the muscles to switch back on. The result is something called sleep paralysis—a temporary feeling when you wake that you are unable to move. Whereas having your muscles turned off while you sleep is normal and happens to everyone, sleep paralysis—waking and still experiencing inhibited muscle movement for a few seconds to a few minutes—is actually considered a sleep disorder, or a parasomnia. Mild or transient forms affect as many as four out of 10 people; however, it only affects about 8 percent of the population to any noticeable extent.

For people with this sleep disorder, it can be a frightening experience. Many researchers attribute certain experiences to sleep paralysis. For example, one theory of nighttime alien abduction is that the sleeper is experiencing sleep paralysis and misinterpreting it. It's also the cause of something called "old hag syndrome"—where someone wakes and believes there's a terrifying supernatural entity sitting on their chest or back, holding them down.

Sleep paralysis can also occur as you're falling asleep, but you're less likely to notice it then because your muscles are in a state of progressive relaxation. It's much more noticeable when you wake suddenly, unable to move. Sleep paralysis can affect how you perceive your dreams. For example, if you've ever woken from a dream trying to scream with nothing coming out, that's likely a transient episode of sleep paralysis.

If you have frequent episodes of sleep paralysis that are disturbing your sleep, you may want to contact your doctor. There are treatments to help you if the condition is frequent and debilitating.

It isn't necessary to address your intention to anyone specific, but you can if you wish. For example, some of my students ask their subconscious, their guides, their guardian angels, or whatever Divine entities they believe in to help.

Release Expectations

Whereas intention drives dream-work, expectation can damage it. Your subconscious will provide the information you most need to know—and this often may not be what you were expecting. Anything can happen in dreams and it's important you maintain an attitude of allowing. That is, remain open to whatever information your subconscious, guide, or higher self shares with you. It is my experience that dreams provide the information we most need in the moment. When we expect them to contain something different, we run the risk of either blocking information that will be beneficial to our well-being or allowing our expectations to create a confirmation bias where we interpret our dreams to mean what we expect and want them to mean instead of what we need to hear.

Expectation creates emotional attachment to an outcome and dreams are like the Wild West of our subconscious. They seldom provide the outcome we're seeking. When we are emotionally attached to an outcome, we may grow frustrated when experience doesn't meet expectation. Be ready to accept what your dreams tell you without trying to force them to fit your expectations.

Anything can happen in dreams and it's important you maintain an attitude of allowing.

SUCCESSFUL SLEEP

If you want to have a vivid and meaningful dream life, it's essential to create an atmosphere that's conducive to sleep. To do this, set up your environment mentally, physically, and energetically in a way that allows you to sleep peacefully, soundly, and comfortably as you dream.

Clearing Your Mind

I used to be a poor sleeper. From the moment I hit the sheets, my mind went a thousand miles per hour, spinning with things that had happened during my day, anxieties, and so many thoughts. It took me years to rectify this. If you also struggle with this, try these fixes that have helped me. They may work for you, too. Understandably, not everyone has time to do everything suggested here but even a few small changes can make a difference.

★ **Meditate before bedtime.** My pre-bedtime meditation is short—five to 10 minutes, depending on the day I've had. I meditate by closing my eyes and focusing on my breath, but you can use any form of meditation that works for you, including guided meditation, affirmations, visualizations, or even just sitting quietly and using a progressive relaxation exercise.

★ **Stay away from screens at least an hour before bed (two hours is optimal).** I know this is difficult in our wired world, but the bigger window of screen-free time you can give yourself before bed, the better chance you'll have of sleeping well. This includes cell phones, television, computers, or any other backlit LCD displays, which have been shown in studies to harm sleep. I actually avoid screens two hours before I go to sleep. I read for about an hour and then I usually take a bath, go through my bedtime routine, and meditate just before I settle down for the night.

★ **Keep it calm.** Avoid stimulating activities an hour or two before bed, such as watching action movies, eating a big meal, or exercising strenuously.

★ **Keep your sleep space sacred.** Use your bedroom only for sex and sleep.

★ **Avoid alcohol or other intoxicants before bedtime.** Although they often make you feel sleepy, ultimately, they harm the quality of your sleep.

★ **If you've never been a great sleeper, consider an affirmation.** Try a statement before sleep confirming deep and comfortable sleep, such as "Tonight I will sleep deeply, comfortably, and peacefully, and I will wake feeling refreshed and energized."

Preserving Your Sleep Space

The atmosphere of your sleep space is also important to peaceful, dream-filled sleep.

What Dreams May Come

Dreaming often happens at night, but that doesn't mean it's the only time you'll have a symbolic dream. Some of my most significant dreams have come to me when I've drifted off to sleep during the day; often during my meditation, which I like to refer to as a "napitation" because I fall asleep more often than I'd like to admit.

Sometimes we fall asleep on plane rides, during car trips, while reading a book, or even sitting on a beach and enjoying the sunlight. And sometimes, dreams come to us during those periods when we haven't prepared and don't have our dream journal handy.

Fortunately, there are some things you can do to help you recall and record those dreams, even if you're not prepared.

* Use the notepad app on your phone and type in a few keywords to help you remember.
* Use a smartphone recorder app and add enough about your dream to help you recall it later.
* Tell someone you're with about the dream as soon as you wake. The act of telling another person will help you remember the dream later.

The trick is somehow to create words to trigger memories so, when you are back at your dream journal, you can remember and start analyzing your dream.

Create an ideal sleep space with the following tips:

★ **Make sure your room temperature is just right.** Ideally, a cooler bedroom and several light layers of blankets work best to maintain the ideal body temperature for sleep.

★ **Make your bed as comfortable as possible.** Have the best mattress you can afford and invest in soft, comfortable sheets and pillows suited to your primary sleep position (back, side, or stomach).

★ **Sleep in light, nonrestrictive clothing.**

★ **Keep the room as dark as you can.** If you have a clock radio, move it away from the bed and adjust the backlight to be as dim as possible. Use blackout shades on your windows to keep ambient light out. Don't use a nightlight.

★ **Keep electronics out of your room.** If you use your cell phone as an alarm, place it across the room instead of right next to you. It's also best not to have a television or computer in the bedroom. If you do, make sure they're turned off.

★ **Place a piece of amethyst next to the bed.** Amethyst is a crystal that supports sleep and dreams.

★ **Consider using a lavender or chamomile essential oil aromatherapy pillow spray, both of which support sleep.** You can also diffuse these essential oils.

★ **Control the sound around you.** Consider using a white noise generator, particularly if outside sounds wake you frequently.

THE PROCESS

I've already supplied some clues to the dream interpretation process in earlier chapters by sharing common contexts as well as meanings of colors, shapes, and numbers. These are all important in dream interpretation, as are other symbols that arise. My dream interpretation process is straightforward and relies highly on intuitive use of the dream symbols. Here's how it works.

Have Your Dream Journal Nearby

As I mentioned, your dream journal doesn't have to be fancy to be useful. It can be a simple notebook or blank journal. Or, if you prefer, you can use your phone's notepad app or voice recorder app. Use any format you like but keep it handy so you can quickly jot down things. If you wake in the middle of the night, a few words are all you need to help you remember.

As soon as you wake, note things in your journal to help you remember the dream.

Rest for a Few Moments

Allow yourself to fully wake before you start interpreting your dreams. You can replay your dream in your head as you do, or just relax. Let yourself come fully awake before taking a deep dive into your dream. Of course, if you wake in the middle of the night, just record your notes quickly and go back to sleep.

Write It Down

Once you are fully awake, write down your entire dream. Be as specific and detailed as possible. The more detail you notice and record, the more accurate your interpretation. Everything you remember from your dream is significant, whether it's someone with a beard or five apples in a bowl. If it stands out to you, it's significant.

Assign Meanings

Once the dream is recorded in all its glory, you can assign meanings and interpret it when you're ready—it doesn't have to be done right away. When you're ready to begin, however, use a dream dictionary or psychic

symbol dictionary and complete the following process.

★ Ask "What do I think this dream means?" Dreams can be really obvious if you stop to think about it for a moment. I find I often know what a dream means before I interpret it, with my interpretation backing it up. If you think you know the meaning of your dream, your intuition is probably correct.

★ Determine the context or the setting of the dream. The dream's context reveals what it's about. This usually has to do either with where the dream takes place or the main action of the dream. For example, if a dream takes place in a hospital, it might be about healing or health, or if you're in a house it may be about your psyche or your body. If it's about fighting, you might feel you are struggling with something right now, or if it's about laughing, you may be finding something joyful or funny in your waking life. Refer to the common contexts in chapter 2 to see if anything there fits, or use another dream dictionary if it's not a context I've provided.

★ Notice the people in your dream. Remember, people in dreams typically represent aspects of you, so ask yourself, "What does this person mean to me, or does this person represent an archetype?" This will tell you the aspects of yourself or your life the dream is about. In some cases, people may represent other people in your life, particularly if it's someone with whom you're close. For example, your child or your spouse may be a representation of that person in waking life.

★ **List numbers and their meanings.** Remember, numbers may be a number you see, hear, or speak, such as asking someone for $45 or seeing the number 404 on a house. It could also be the number of something you've noticed, such as five golf balls or three dogs. The number will likely tell you something about the symbol it appears in conjunction with. For example, if you see a door with the number three on it, the door may represent an opportunity and the number three would suggest it is a creative opportunity (see the chart in chapter 2, page 44), and so on.

★ **List colors and their meanings.** Like numbers, colors provide deeper insight. For instance, if you're wearing something in a shade of red, it might suggest the face you're presenting to the public is one of passion and sexuality, whereas a yellow shade may show you're trying to present a public face of self-esteem and confidence.

★ **List shapes and their meanings.** Shapes that stand out may be significant. For example, if you notice geometric patterns in wallpaper or you spot an object with a particular shape that's unusual for that object, then it may be telling you more about that symbol. For instance, a heart-shaped doorway may suggest romantic opportunity, or a spiral pathway may mean your path in life is unfolding in a certain way.

★ **Record other symbols in as much detail as possible.** Any other things that appear in dreams, such as objects, animals, or vehicles, are all fodder for your interpretation. Notice as much detail about them as you can so you can create as rich an interpretation as possible. Look them up in your dream dictionary and record one or two of the possible meanings that feel the most on point to you.

★ **Use the plot to pull it together.** Finally, once you've recorded all the symbols and determined potential meanings for them, notice how the symbols interact with the action or plot of the dream. What are you doing with the objects you see? How are you using them? How do you feel about them? All these clues help you pull together the symbols into a coherent dream that provides valuable information.

MAKING CONNECTIONS

I've mentioned before that dream interpretation is highly intuitive. For the most accurate reading of a dream, use your insight into your knowledge and understanding of yourself to arrive at the dream's meaning. Doing so can help you discern what a dream means when you've got more than one definition for a dream symbol or when you're struggling to decide whether the symbol represents something from personal symbolism or the collective consciousness.

What's Happening in Your Life?

First, compare the symbols to what's happening in your life right now. Often, it's easy to see how a dream dovetails with where you are in your life and what you're experiencing. For instance, when I was learning to practice Reiki, I had a dream about lightning bolts coming out of my hands. It was easy to realize this dream was about my work with Reiki and energy healing.

There's Only You in Your Dreams

As I've mentioned, our subconscious mind tends to be pretty darn self-centered. Assume that everything and everyone in your dream is telling you something about you unless you have a good reason to believe otherwise. For example, when I was pregnant with my son, I kept dreaming about a baby. It was easy for me to recognize the baby in my dreams wasn't actually about me; it was about the baby I would have in my life in a few short months. As an interesting aside, I had many of those dreams, all with the same baby, and when my son was born, he looked exactly like the baby in my dreams. A mother's intuition is an amazing thing.

Identifying Archetypes

Archetypal energies show up in our lives at different times. Pay attention to the archetypes and relate them to your current needs, experiences, or desires. For example, if you've been feeling down and a motherly female figure shows up, chances are it's the Great Mother archetype (see page 39) coming to provide nurturing and comfort. If you've been wandering a spiritual path and feeling lost or unfocused and then encounter a guru in your dream, there's a good chance it's the Wise One archetype (see page 38) come to provide support and guidance on your path.

Your Dream Landscape

Although dream settings and contexts can be symbolic, they can also be personal. For example, if you're an airline pilot and you dream about an airplane, it's probably a dream about career as opposed to a symbolic airplane dream. If you are a bird-watcher and you dream about birds, it could be that your dream is about hobbies as opposed to the typical interpretation of birds, which is about aspirations. If you're a teacher and dream about school, chances are it's a work dream (or a stress dream) instead of being a dream about needing to learn something.

When Symbols Aren't Symbols

Likewise, if a symbol has a personal meaning to you, such as something you use in your daily life or job, chances are it's about what you use it for as opposed to its symbolic meaning. For example, I am a musician and sound healer and work with various instruments, such as singing bowls and bells, on a regular basis. So, although a bell in a dream symbolically represents a warning or a call to do something, to me, it's probably about work, music, healing, or teaching. Likewise, a technical support person who dreams about malfunctioning technology is likely dreaming about work as opposed to the inability to communicate with someone. A needle for a seamstress probably doesn't mean a relationship needs mending, although a shirt might. A pill for a doctor doesn't mean it's necessarily about healing; it's probably about work, and so on.

When Symbols Are Personal

Personal symbolism also plays a very important role in dreams. For example, if you grew up Muslim, your symbolism will be quite different from someone who is pagan, and that person's symbolism is different from Christian symbolism.

Personal symbols come from culture, family, neighborhood, educational background, religion, racial affiliation, and more. For example, if you're of Chinese heritage, you may view a rat, which is a sign of the Chinese zodiac, differently from someone from the West, who would see the rat as a pest. Likewise, if you're

Native American or First Nation, you may have different associations for totem or spirit animals than a non-native. If you're Catholic, incense in a dream may mean something totally different to you than it would to a New Age believer or a feng shui practitioner.

I always suggest seeking personal associations for symbols before you look to universal symbols. Ask yourself what a symbol means in regard to your personal life, family, neighborhood or community, friends, educational affiliations, hobbies, work or career, city, state, region, country, race, culture, spiritual background or religion, gender identity, sexual orientation, political affiliation or beliefs, etc. It's important to realize how much each can affect how you view a symbol. Look there before looking universally.

Dreaming Is Personal

Ultimately, dreaming is highly personal, and you know yourself better than anyone else does. Dream dictionaries can get you in the ballpark about a dream's meaning, but it's up to you to personalize it as much as possible. Doing so brings you deeper understanding of yourself and provides guidance to help you move forward in life.

Exploring Dreams

To truly understand the dream interpretation process in action, we're going to interpret several dreams in the next section. I'll walk you through, step by step, so you can understand exactly how to arrive at an interpretation.

Occam's razor is a principle of logic that suggests that, all things being equal, the simplest explanation is usually the correct one. This is true in dream interpretation. Look to simple explanations first; if those make sense to you, they are most likely correct.

FOUR DREAMS INTERPRETED

Let's look at some of the dreams I've interpreted to help you understand the process.

Some of the details and personally identifying information of the dreamers have been omitted and names have been changed to protect privacy.

Note: I often interpret dreams people write blindly in to my column. That is, the dream is sent anonymously and I don't know anything about the person. However, for the dreams that follow, the dreamer contacted me after my interpretation to thank me and tell me how accurate it was, explaining what led to the dream or what it was about after the fact.

Dreamer #1: Ali

Ali is a 40-year-old mother of a teenage son. She had this dream following the 2016 presidential election. Ali self-identifies as a Democrat and liberal and she is a spiritual teacher.

Ali's Dream

We have a party for a female friend who looks haggard and will not speak with me. Bill and Hillary Clinton are there. Bill knows who I am. As we go to get food on an escalator, I ask him to take a picture with my dog and he obliges. Later, I take a picture of Hillary. Instead of using my phone, I use a key fob that I can't get pictures off. When I return after getting food, the Clintons are gone (they indicated they would need to leave early), so I can't get another picture, but I will get it off my key fob.

There is a row of flags across the water and people are going by to place them in flag holders, so they stretch entirely across the water. I have a flag that is kind of a cross between Israel's and Greece's flags, and I swim to place it in the flag holder about halfway across the space.

What we're looking for:

In Ali's dream, we want to look at the following:

★ **Context:** A party for a friend, later in the water
★ **People:** Bill and Hillary Clinton, female friend who looks tired
★ **Numbers, colors, and shapes:** None noted
★ **Symbols:** Food, escalator, dog, key fob, flag holders, flag
★ **Plot:** Friend won't talk to Ali, taking pictures, swimming across water

Interpretation and resolution:

The context is a party, which, in this case, has a literal translation to political party. Later, the water represents emotions or the subconscious mind.

People in dreams represent aspects of Ali.

★ **Friend who looks exhausted.** Ali may be feeling tired or overworked.
★ **Bill and Hillary Clinton.** Politicians, political archetypes, liberals, Democrats

The significant symbols in the dream have the following meanings:

★ **Food:** Food refers to thoughts, ideas, and feelings.

★ **Escalator:** An escalator shows movement from one level of consciousness to another (spiritual journey). The thoughts and ideas (food) are up the next level of consciousness (escalator).

★ **Fob:** I'm not aware of an interpretation for a key fob; however, a fob is a type of key, just more technologically advanced. A key is a keeper of secrets, or it locks away secrets. So, in a dream, a key symbolizes access to ideas, knowledge, etc.

★ **Flags:** Flagpoles represent stability, whereas flags represent peace and prosperity.

The significance of the dream's plot points is symbolic as well:

★ **Friend isn't speaking to Ali:** Ali is ignoring or overlooking some part of herself.

★ **Taking photos:** Dreaming of taking a picture suggests the need to focus on an idea or issue.

★ **Swimming:** Ali is moving through or exploring emotions or her subconscious.

The dream represents Ali's political ideals and how they relate to her spirituality. At the time of the dream, Ali was feeling frustrated and exhausted in relation to politics, and there was part of her that was angry at herself for the current situation. Ali was struggling to integrate a political situation with her spiritual beliefs and aspirations. The dream was telling her the way to do this existed in her subconscious mind; it was there for the taking when she was ready to find it, even though it felt like a struggle. The dream told Ali to continue to explore her thoughts and feelings and pay attention to her deeper emotions about the issues so she could arrive at a place of peace with current politics and find a way to balance her ideals with what was happening in the world. The dream was also reminding Ali that she was the source of her own stability and prosperity and telling her she'd be okay regardless of what happened politically.

When Ali wrote back after the dream interpretation, she told me she was finally able to find peace about politics that weren't working to her liking by delving deeper into spiritual practices and sending love instead of anger to a political system she believes is broken.

Dreamer #2: Jorge

Jorge is a 40-something father. When he had this dream he and his wife were in a difficult spot in their marriage after she had been unfaithful.

Jorge's Dream

I was having another one of my typical whacky dreams about the television show Game of Thrones *when it suddenly cut to this very clear image of a younger woman with short dirty-blond hair, a light complexion with some mild acne, and wearing glasses. She looked kind of like an old girlfriend of mine. She got right into my face and spoke the following to me—it was very clear and I knew it was French—"Marin Quan." This was how I heard it but after doing a bit of research, I think the correct spelling is "Maurin Quina."*

What we're looking for:

Jorge's dream is unusual because it contained a phrase that required some research, "Maurin Quina." There wasn't a lot to go on, but there was still enough there to interpret. In Jorge's dream, we want to look at the following:

★ Context: *Game of Thrones*, which was interrupted by the woman with a message
★ People: Younger blond woman with acne and glasses
★ Numbers, colors, and shapes: None noted

★ Symbols: Maurin Quina
★ Plot: Woman interrupting *Game of Thrones* and getting in Jorge's face speaking these words to him

Interpretation and resolution:

To interpret Jorge's dream, I had to research the phrase Maurin Quina and *Game of Thrones* (I've never seen it.). I found the phrase on a liqueur poster depicting a green devil with a grin on his face holding a bottle of absinthe.

★ Context: *Game of Thrones* is a fantasy show, so the woman is interrupting Jorge's fantasy to give him a powerful message.
★ People: A light-skinned, blond-haired, blue-eyed woman is often representative of the archetype Divine Child (see page 38), which represents innocence and goodness. In the Christian faith, this archetype is personified by the Baby Jesus. The fact that this archetype has acne shows there may be some flaws or self-consciousness associated with this image. Eyeglasses indicate a lack of clear vision.
★ Symbols: Maurin Quina—see following.

I interpreted Maurin Quina based on the poster I'd found.

- ★ **The color green (the color of the devil in Maurin Quina) actually indicates positive change.** It is also the color of the heart chakra and can, therefore, indicate love, or it may indicate "going green" and being more natural. Alternatively, it can symbolize jealousy, envy, or wealth.
- ★ **Absinthe is a green liquor and can, therefore, have all the same symbolism as the color green.** It's also associated in dreams with frivolity or foolishness.
- ★ **The devil (or green fairy) in the advertisement may be a representation of the trickster archetype.** This archetype (see page 38) is a symbol of duality, of playing tricks, of frivolity, and of things not being as they seem. Alternatively, the devil can represent deception.

Jorge was being given a message to look past a fantasy he held and explore the reality of a situation instead. The dream had a few symbols about frivolity and foolishness. It was telling him all was not as it seemed, and that what seemed foolish or frivolous might actually have a deeper significance that Jorge wasn't able to see clearly. He was focused on the frivolous instead of dealing with what was right in front of him. Focusing on the true issue instead of fantasy would help him move forward and bring positive change into his life.

Jorge wrote me later that he'd been trying to escape the realities of his difficult marriage when he had the dream and the dream interpretation reminded him he needed to focus on the reality of what had happened in his marriage, so he could choose whether to move forward with his wife or move on.

Dreamer #3: Salima

Salima is a graphic artist who came to her career later in life. When she was in her twenties, she worked in a very busy doctor's office as a receptionist.

Salima's Dream

I am at the doctor's office where I used to work. Some crime has occurred there and it was committed by one of the employees. We've just gotten back some of our financial books from the police relating to that employee. Patients start to come in and I am scrambling to keep up with all of the requirements on a very busy day. The number of patients is overwhelming. At the same time, a toilet overflows with disgusting water flooding the office floor.

Salima's dream wasn't rich on detail, but it provides a good look at how to interpret dreams in which there aren't as many details, but these details still seem significant.

★ **Context:** A doctor's office, former job
★ **People:** Many patients
★ **Color, numbers, shapes:** Nothing stood out
★ **Symbols:** Police, crime, toilet, feces, and urine
★ **Plot:** Busy day, police and criminal activity, overflowing toilet

Interpretation and resolution:
The symbols in Salima's dreams were fairly classic symbols from the collective consciousness.

★ **Context:** A doctor's office is a place of healing. A former job represents a lesson that may still need to be learned. Theft indicates loss. In this case, the loss was at an old job, so Salima may have felt she'd lost a lesson that still needed to be learned.
★ **People:** There were a lot of them, though none stood out except for how overwhelming they were. Salima's dream meant she felt overwhelmed.
★ **Symbols:** Overflowing toilet is a release of emotions; urine and feces are about cleansing; toilet is also about cleansing

This dream indicated a desire for cleansing, purification, healing, and unification with spirit, but Salima's ego was fighting it. Her ego desperately wanted to retain a sense of separation, but her spirit yearned for integration. Salima's dream was telling her that her ego would continue to make noise as long as she paid attention to it and allowed it to overwhelm her. Instead of fighting her ego, the dream suggested she embrace it to help her ego realize that, even as she further integrated with spirit, she would retain her sense of self.

Salima realized after this dream it was time to quiet her internal struggle. She began to meditate and worked on several self-healing practices whenever her ego acted up, and soon she moved into a more spiritual place in her life.

Dreamer #4: Kelly

Kelly is in her late forties. She had been laid off from work and was feeling disconnected and unsure of where to go in her life.

Kelly's Dream

In my dream, I wake to find my right leg has been tattooed from the knee down. I'm furious and the people around me keep telling me to calm down because it's not permanent ink. The tattoo is a series of lines and weird-looking hieroglyphics I could not understand. The only symbol I could recall is a tree with a swirl in the leaves. It was the most prominent item.

As the week progresses, before I go to sleep, I tell myself I need help to understand whether this is important and about the meaning of the tattoo. A few nights later I am walking with a man known to me in the dream but not in reality. I'm telling him about the tattoo and he introduces me to another man. He tells me that if anyone can figure out the meaning, it would be him. He asks me to sketch it and he will work on interpreting it.

What we're looking for:

Kelly's dream didn't even make any pretext of not being symbolic. It told her—in no uncertain terms—it contained symbols and it was up to her to figure out what they meant.

★ **Context:** Waking from a dream and then dreaming again

★ **People:** Two men trying to figure out the meaning of the tattoo

★ **Colors, numbers, shapes:** Two (men)

★ **Symbols:** Tattoo, tree, leaves, hieroglyphics, right leg

★ **Plot:** Getting an impermanent tattoo, anger about the tattoo, trying to find the meaning of the tattoo

Interpretation and resolution:

A deep dive into the symbols reveals what Kelly's dream is about:

★ **Context:** Dreaming about dreaming and waking is telling Kelly the dream is significant.

★ **People:** Two men; probably spirit guides

★ **Colors, numbers, shapes:** Two represents duality and partnership

★ **Symbols:** Tattoos are about individuality or standing out; dreams are about growth and hope, leg (the location of the tattoo) is about standing up for yourself or standing on your own two feet; right side (her right leg) is about conscious reality; leaves represent making improvements in life and hieroglyphics symbolize discovering one's path.

★ **Plot:** The plot is about trying to find out what the message from the dream is; it's telling her this is important and she needs to understand it.

Taken together, the dream suggested Kelly was seeking her individual path in life—one that allowed her to control her destiny through deliberate choices and actions. Although Kelly sought to make improvements, she also faced obstacles that frustrated her. Her higher self wanted to remind her, however, that this state of flux was impermanent (the tattoo was impermanent). The guides were telling her to be patient so she could move through and reach a new beginning where she was able to stand on her own two feet.

DEVELOPING YOUR PRACTICE

Dream interpretation takes practice and requires time and consistent effort. I've gotten progressively better at dream interpretation over the years and, as I have, I've been better able to use the content of my dreams to serve my highest and greatest good. You can also bring your dreams into other practices in your life to foster growth and change.

Psychoanalysis

Many people wishing to make changes in their life try psychoanalysis. Dream interpretation is a significant piece of the psychoanalytic puzzle. Discussing your dreams and interpretations with a therapist trained in dream analysis can help you gain deeper insight into yourself, providing a plan of action to grow and change, which can help you release parts of yourself you hold in shadow.

If you wish to work with a therapist in psychoanalysis, discuss your dreams with them and then offer your interpretation. However, keep an open mind because your therapist may have insights that hadn't occurred to you.

Problem Solving

Dreams offer a powerful means of problem solving. I often go to sleep with a specific problem on my mind and wake with a solution. For example, when my son was a senior in high school and accepted to college, I had absolutely no idea how we were going to pay for it. Needless to say, I was a bit stressed. Each night before I went to sleep, I asked for help with this particular situation. One night about a week in, I had a dream I was standing in front of a classroom teaching. At the time, I hadn't taught anything for years. The last thing I'd taught was aerobics back in the late '80s and early '90s! But many people had been asking me to teach classes based on my books and I just never thought it was an option. Ultimately, teaching classes became one of several

Interpretation Best Practices

Hopefully you feel ready to start interpreting your dreams. Following are some best practices to help you get an accurate read on what your dreams mean.

You are the focus of your dream. Always start with that assumption and interpret based on that.

Nobody knows the dreamer better than you do. Although seeking dream interpretation or input from others can help if you feel stuck, nobody has as much insight into you as you do, even if you don't realize it. Listen to your intuition before you listen to someone else's.

Look to personal experiences and filters first. We all have our own unique way of seeing the world that causes us to filter everything—including dream experiences—through our personal filters. Therefore, you should always ask what you think the dream means before you do anything else.

Keep an open mind. Allow for guidance to come through in your dreams; often dreams can make us open our eyes to things we can't or won't see in our waking life.

Don't force it. If you're just not getting a dream interpretation, take a break and try again later.

Sometimes a dream doesn't have meaning, or it doesn't have a meaning you can discern right now. Look at it later and if it still doesn't come, leave it in your dream journal. At some point, something may arise that will provide a key to interpreting it.

solutions that allowed us to pay for my son's college expenses without going into debt.

Your dreams can help you solve problems you're aware you have and, more frequently, problems you may not even realize you have. Mine have pointed me toward health issues, and showed me when I was holding onto unhealthy emotions, and helped me realize when I was sticking with something that no longer served me. I've reorganized my entire house because dreams showed me that a different arrangement would facilitate better energy flow, discovered issues in my relationships, and more.

Ask for help in your dreams. It may not always come in the form you expect, but if you're worrying about a problem, ask about it before going to sleep. Stay with it but keep an open mind and don't have expectations. Note the help you ask for in your dream journal so you don't forget you've asked for it. Be patient and willing to accept unconventional solutions to your problems in the form of dreams.

Get to Know Yourself

When you delve into the content of your dreams, you get to know someone you may have thought you knew everything about but really didn't: you. We all have things about ourselves we

would rather not acknowledge. We each have aspects of our personalities we don't love, behaviors we know don't serve us, and emotions we don't want to acknowledge. Our dreams provide an unflinching look at the true us.

Peering so deeply into yourself can be uncomfortable, but it's eminently worthwhile. Dreams shine a bright light into the darkest corners of self. There's an analogy I use in my classes when people start to get uncomfortable with what their dreams might reveal to them. I remind them of this: If you're in a dark basement with the lights off and you can't see in front of you, it can be scary. Maybe you hear a scraping noise in the corner and your imagination runs wild. You're terrified of what is there. Maybe it's an animal or a murderer. But when you turn on the overhead light and it illuminates that dark, cobweb-filled corner where you heard the sound, you might see the air vent overhead that's causing a piece of cardboard to flap against a wall and make the scraping sound. Suddenly, it's no longer scary.

Our internal dark corners are a lot like that. They seem far scarier than they actually are because we keep them dark hoping nobody will notice our flaws. But when you have a dream and boldly examine what the dream is telling you, it's like flipping on the light switch. Suddenly, that terrifying thing you were afraid of in your deepest, darkest self starts to look ordinary and not even a little frightening.

I know this because my dreams have caused me to flip on that light switch many times and I've always discovered that my fear of what was hiding in the dark was far worse, more painful, and more destructive than what was actually there.

Staying the Course

It may take time to become proficient at remembering dreams, recognizing what is significant in them, and interpreting them. I developed my ability over years of regular practice until it became second nature to me. Now it's my party trick. People ask me what something means, and after I ask, "What do *you* think it means?" I can quickly offer a synopsis. I learned to do this by interpreting many of my own dreams. You can make interpreting dreams your party trick, too. Or, you can use it more privately by using your dreams to get to know yourself. Put in consistent effort. If you get stuck, take a break and come back to it. Make it something that's fun instead of a

chore. Turn it into a practice, something like yoga or meditation, in which you take time to do something just for you.

Start with a simple dream. Give it a try and see what you come up with. Then, when you're comfortable with simple dreams, try something more complex. Delve deeper. Make the process yours. Chances are, you'll discover that, with regular practice, you'll soon be interpreting your dreams like a pro.

BEAUTIFUL DREAMER

Dream interpretation is a fascinating process. Sometimes it's a lot of fun, and other times it takes a bit more work. Often, it's surprising. Always, it's enlightening. When you delve into the landscape of your dreams and find what your dreams reveal, you'll discover a new road map to yourself. You'll learn what motivates you, what frightens you, where you're succeeding, and where you might need some work.

Dreams are a powerful tool for healing. I know people who have healed relationships based on dreams. I know people who have gained better understanding of why they struggle with certain things. I know others who have found a way to forgive someone—perhaps even themselves—because of what they learned while they slept.

Dreams provide a window into the most important person in your life: you. They reveal your gifts and your challenges, your joys and your sorrows. They allow you to process difficult emotions. They provide the opportunity to communicate with people you've lost. They allow you to experience things you can't experience in the waking world, such as flying alongside a flock of birds or riding across the ocean on the back of a whale. They offer access to your subconscious mind and your higher self. They introduce you to guides and guardians.

They allow you to grow spiritually, emotionally, and mentally. It's miraculous that all this happens while you sleep.

When you wake, take a moment to recall your dreams. Then, with it fresh in your mind, write it in your journal. Grab a cup of tea, curl up in a comfy chair, and follow the process. Use the dictionary entries in the next section or use one of the resources I provide (see page 110). Take your time and be kind to yourself. Dream-work is the work of you and it offers insight into a whole world just waiting to be explored.

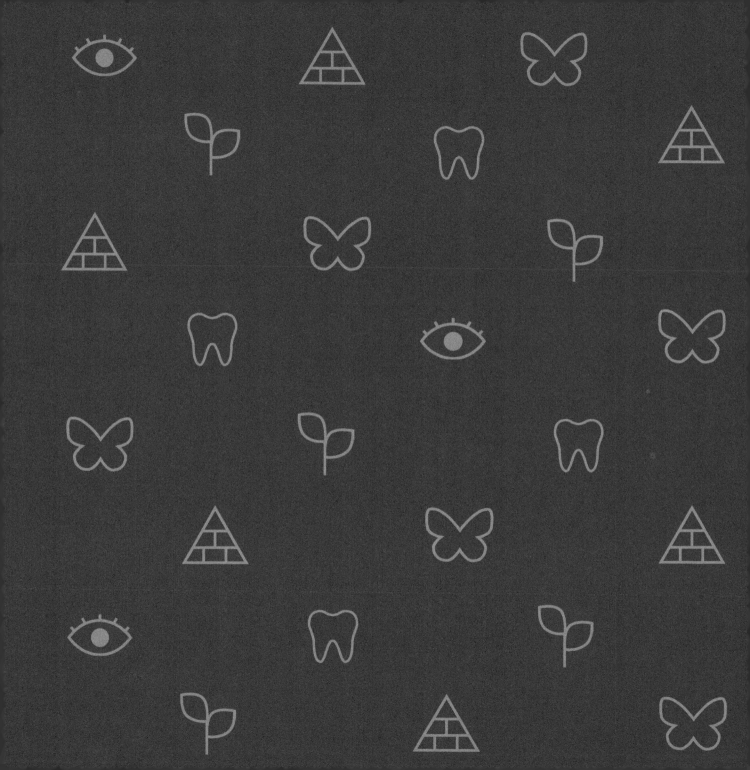

Part II
DREAM DICTIONARY

HOW TO USE THIS DREAM DICTIONARY (AND OTHERS)

I own a variety of dream dictionaries and dictionaries of psychic symbols and they are all different. The definitions they provide are similar but there is some variation from book to book. Likewise, in the definitions that follow, I strive to give the most commonsense interpretations, but you'll notice that for many entries I offer more than one choice about the meaning of that symbol. In my classes, one of the first things people ask me is how to resolve these differences. The truth is, it's up to you, the dreamer, to resolve them. Read through and see which feels right to you. Try each definition in the context of your dream and see which one makes the most sense for who you are, how you feel, and what you're experiencing right now. Although there are symbols and archetypes that are part of the collective consciousness, keep in mind we each see these uniquely through our own filters based on childhood associations, family traditions, culture, religious background, racial background, regional influences, and so on.

You'll find that although I stick to the most commonsense, logical explanations in this dictionary, occasionally I'll relate the definitions to other traditions, such as the concept of yin and yang in Taoism, symbols in tarot, those found in Chinese and Western astrology, and various religious or philosophical traditions.

When you're interpreting your dreams, always start by asking, "What does this mean to me?" before you look up the symbol. You'll find your instincts are usually pretty close because there's really not as much mystery in dream symbols as people think. Read the following definitions and you'll see what I mean.

ANIMALS

Animals play many roles in dreams. Because they are such a big part of our world, they are also a part of the dream world. Ask yourself what the animal represents to you before you look to universal symbols. You may find animal symbolism in things that are meaningful to you, such as Chinese or Western astrology or Native American and First Nation totems and spirit animals. If you're afraid of an animal, it may mean something different than if you love that animal. For example, snakes are one of my phobias, but my son and his girlfriend love snakes and have one, named Norbert, as a pet. The meaning of snakes in my dreams will likely be very different from the meaning of snakes in theirs. Likewise, if you love dogs but dislike cats, these two animals will mean something different than someone who loves cats and hates dogs.

Alligator/Crocodile

Both alligators and crocodiles have notoriously thick skin. They're also cunning and deceptive as they lurk near the banks of bodies of water and await their victims. They are frightening and dangerous creatures. Seeing either in a dream usually has one of two meanings: you are too thick skinned or you're overly sensitive. It might also indicate you are being deceitful in some aspect of your life, someone is deceiving you, or you're deceiving yourself. Likewise, it could suggest danger is lurking and you should proceed with caution.

Ant

Ants are industrious workers, but they are also just a cog in a giant machine of other ants serving their queen. Recognizing these qualities will help you understand what an ant means when it appears in a dream. An ant in a dream indicates the need to put your head down and work harder, or it may suggest you feel like a small, impersonal piece in a giant machine that is taking without giving anything back. These dreams are often about how you feel about your work life. It may suggest you're working hard but feel underappreciated, or that you feel you're putting in substantial work and effort but not being noticed for it.

Bee

A bee's primary job is to work hard and gather pollen to bring back to the hive. That pollen becomes honey, which helps the bees survive during winter. Seeing a bee in a dream suggests hard work and a payoff for that effort. It reminds you if you work hard, you will be rewarded in some way—often financially, but in other ways as well.

If it's not a bee you see, but a wasp or a yellow jacket, the dream is about anger or aggression—yours or somebody else's. Wasps and yellow jackets have a sharp sting when they feel threatened and you may feel threatened in your waking life and are reacting with a stinging emotion.

Bird

Birds, which enjoy the freedom to soar high above the rest of the world, often represent lofty goals and ambitions, or the joy of freedom.

To learn more about what specific birds represent, pay attention to the color of their feathers, whether or not they fly, and if you're happy or frightened to see them. If the bird is a crow, for instance, and it makes you uncomfortable, it may reflect your shadow or aspects of yourself you choose to keep hidden.

Bug

In colloquial English, we often ask people what's bothering them by saying, "Is something bugging you?" Bugs are symbolic of this. They represent the things we worry and fret about, so when they appear in your dream, they suggest you feel stressed about something. Pay attention to the type of bug, its colors, and how you feel about it as well as the context in which it appears. These things will help you determine what's bugging you.

If the bug becomes a moth or a butterfly, it represents creativity, growth, and transformation. Your dream is saying you can turn your worries into something beautiful through creativity or personal growth. If it's a ladybug, it represents luck and good fortune.

Cat

Some pet lovers will tell you that dogs are like men and cats are like women. Keeping this in mind, cats in dreams represent the concept of yin: dark, mysterious, secretive, feminine, intuitive, and independent. Pay attention to the cat's color and behavior as well as how you feel about the cat. If you're not a fan of cats, for example, the dream may represent feeling overly secretive or duplicitous. If you love cats, the dream may be about the more positive expressions of yin, such as intuition or femininity. Due to the common superstition about black cats, a black cat may represent inauspicious luck.

Dog

Anyone who has ever had a dog as a pet will tell you that dogs are among the most loyal companions a person can have. They are also trusting and protective. This is exactly what dogs represent in dreams: loyalty, protection, and trust. If the dog is vicious in a dream, it may be that you feel protective or in need of protection, or it may be that you are angry your loyalty has gone unrewarded or your trust has been broken by someone. Being bitten by a dog in a dream means you feel someone you thought was loyal to you or trustworthy has betrayed you in some way.

Dolphin/Whale

Cetaceans (dolphins, whales, and porpoises) are believed by many to be the earthly keepers of the Akashic records, which are the spiritual records of every life souls have lived, are living now, and will live. The Akashic records contain the wisdom of the ages. When they appear in dreams, cetaceans represent wisdom and guidance from a higher source, or they may be the representation of your karma arising from many lifetimes. Their appearance in dreams often indicates you have latent psychic abilities. Pay special attention to these dreams, as they exist to guide you along your spiritual path.

Elephant

Elephants never forget. And remembering this is the key to understanding an elephant when it appears in your dreams. Elephants in dreams are often a sign you're living in the past, holding onto a memory too tightly, or that you're allowing something from the past to keep you from moving forward. Elephants signify the need to let go of—not the need to forget—memories that are holding you back.

Elephants are also powerful and strong, so their appearance in a dream could represent personal power and strength or the need for strength and courage.

In the Hindu tradition, Ganesha, the remover of obstacles, is half elephant and half human (elephant head on a human body). If Ganesha appears in your dreams, it may suggest ways to overcome obstacles you currently face.

Fish

Fish live under the water and, if you recall from the context section, water represents emotions, so fish represent what lies beneath those emotions. In dreams, fish tell you that things you have buried in your subconscious are rising to the surface. Pay attention to the color of the fish, which can tell you more about the emotions you are experiencing.

In Taoist and feng shui traditions, koi fish (carp) represent prosperity and wealth. Dreaming of koi could predict prosperity and wealth, indicate that you desire wealth,

or represent the feeling it has eluded you, depending on the context.

Horse

Horses are physically powerful and strong. They are also wild animals that have to be tamed to function as humans would like them to. A horse in your dreams suggests you may need to tame some of your wilder urges, or significant power and strength. Wild horses or horses running could symbolize freedom or the desire for freedom. If it's a donkey and not a horse, it suggests you or someone else is being obstinate.

Lion

When I see a lion, my first thought is of the cowardly lion in the film *The Wizard of Oz*. Powerful and ferocious, everyone was scared of the lion even though he, himself, was seeking courage. The next thing that comes to mind is that lions are the King of the Jungle. Both images factor into the symbolic meaning of lions in a dream. They may represent power and absolute authority; they may represent fear of something you feel is more powerful than you; or they may represent courage.

Lizard

Humans are thinking, reasoning creatures, but we all have something called a "lizard brain," which is our instinctive, unthinking self. Lizards in dreams represent these instinctual behaviors and appetites, such as for food, drink, or sex. Lizards are also reptiles with "cold blood," so a lizard may also represent cruel, unthinking, or casual behavior, or it may suggest someone is treating you poorly.

If the lizard is a chameleon, it suggests you are able to change and adapt to any situation.

Monkey

There is an expression, "the monkey on your back," which means a problem that seems difficult to solve or even insurmountable. Monkeys in dreams may represent such problems. Other symbols in the dream and its plot and context should tell you more about what troubles you.

Monkeys are also playful and fun to watch, so if a monkey appears in your dream and you're delighted by its antics, it might suggest it's time to lighten up and have some fun. Alternatively, a monkey could represent playfulness or humor.

Mouse/Rat

Mice are tiny, often hidden creatures we don't think about unless they somehow get our attention by, say, darting across our living room floor! Mice in dreams may indicate that you feel hidden or insignificant and that it may be time to do something to get noticed.

Rats in dreams are a bit more malevolent. When we call someone a "rat," we refer to a less than desirable character, often someone who is duplicitous. Rats in dreams often suggest that you worry someone will betray you in some way, or that they present one face to you but behave differently otherwise.

Owl

If you've heard the expression "wise old owl," you will immediately recognize what owls represent in our dreams: wisdom and awareness. Their appearance in a dream may suggest wise guidance, or that it's time to be more aware to see something you're missing. They may also indicate you need to learn from experience.

For some people, owls are almost mystical and so may also represent spiritual insight, magic, or a mystical experience.

Pig

Pigs are considered dirty animals that roll around in the muck, and when we eat too much, we say we feel like a pig. This is what pigs represent in our dreams: filth, the willingness to "roll around in the mud" or "get down and dirty," and greed or hedonism run amok. They might also represent other piggish things, such as gluttony, sloth, and stubbornness.

In Chinese astrology, however, pigs are an auspicious symbol, so in dreams they could represent positive things, such as success and abundance.

Rabbit

A rabbit's foot is considered a lucky symbol in Western culture. Rabbits are also known for their abundant breeding and multiplying. Rabbits in dreams represent either (or both) of these concepts: luck and abundance or sexuality and fertility (often excessive). If a rabbit appears in a dream, it may indicate luck is on the way or you feel lucky.

In dreams, rabbits multiplying quickly may show that minimal efforts will have huge payoffs and exponential rewards. It can also be a sign of growth, birth, creation, and new energy.

Scorpion

The first thing that probably comes to mind regarding a scorpion is its sting—and this is exactly what a scorpion signifies in a dream. It may represent that you feel stung by something someone has said or done, or that your behavior is stinging and painful to another. It could also indicate you fear someone is going to hurt you.

In astrology, scorpions represent the sign Scorpio, which is a water sign. This represents depth, secrecy, and deep emotion, which is often our negative emotions, such as jealousy, envy, and anger.

Shark

Sharks are predators, often thought of as cunning, hostile, and deceitful. A shark in a dream suggests you feel someone is behaving in a predatory way toward you, or that you are behaving in a sharklike manner. Because sharks swim underwater, which represents emotion, sharks in dreams suggest your emotional behavior is predatory, or you feel someone is treating you in an emotionally predatory manner.

Sharks can also represent ruthlessness, anger, or greed. If the shark attacks you, it may suggest you feel overcome by these emotions or you feel under relentless attack by someone in your life who is predatory.

Snake

Fear of snakes is one of the most common phobias. (As noted earlier, I am terrified of them.) Snakes in dreams represent your fears, often fears you may not realize you have. The term "snake in the grass" indicates someone that hides, lying in wait to spring on you and do you harm. A snake may suggest you feel someone is lying in wait and will betray you soon.

In Chinese astrology, the snake represents the yin part of chi energy, so snakes may also represent yin qualities such as mystery, intuition, and darkness.

Freud, not surprisingly, believed snakes in dreams represented sexual energy and libido.

Spider

Spiders spin intricate webs; they are creative animals. Spiders in dreams often represent creativity, although if you are afraid of spiders they may represent your fears as well. We also refer to things such as "spinning a web of deceit," so spiders may indicate you are being deceived or deceitful in your dealings with others.

Spiders sit in their webs away from others, watching and waiting. Because of this, they are often outside observers instead of active participants. In classic dream interpretation, spiders have this meaning: You feel like an outsider looking in, or you feel somehow disconnected from certain aspects of your life.

Turtle/Tortoise

Turtles and tortoises live a long time. They are also often thought of as wise, perhaps because of their wise-looking faces. In dreams, turtles often represent these two qualities: wisdom and longevity.

Turtles also carry their shelter with them at all times. When they sense danger, they can withdraw into their shell. Sometimes turtles in dreams represent shelter and safety.

Turtles are also notoriously slow and in dreams may represent a period of slowing down, the need to slow down, or a time when progress will be slow and steady.

Wolf

Wolves are viewed by many as highly spiritual animals. We also have associations such as "lone wolf" and "wolf pack." Often a wolf in your dream may represent magic and spirituality, or it may represent solitude.

Because wolves run in packs, they are also incredibly loyal animals and their appearance in dreams may suggest loyalty and protection.

If you dream of a werewolf, it's showing you that someone or something presents itself as one thing, but is really something else.

Worm

We tend to think of worms as something icky and we even refer to unsavory people as worms. These associations are powerful and give you an idea of what worms represent when they appear in your dreams. They represent a low station in life, someone who is crawling around in the mud because of their actions and attitudes. They may indicate you are feeling degraded in some way, or they may indicate someone is being a "worm," that is, being deceitful.

If the worm is a caterpillar, it represents a stage of life before a transition or metamorphosis. This dream can suggest you are changing or about to transform in a vital way.

ITEMS/THINGS

Items and things can be quite symbolic. However, personal associations usually trump the universal dream symbols. So, when an object appears in the dream, before turning to a dream dictionary (or using this one), always ask, "What does this mean to me?" As with animals, we may have different associations depending on our background. For instance, I grew up in the church so the Bible, to me, represents a source of spiritual wisdom, but if you grew up as a Buddhist it probably doesn't. If you fear guns, chances are guns will have a negative connotation in a dream. If you are comfortable with them, there's a good chance the association will be more positive.

Bible

In Western culture, particularly Christian Western culture, the Bible is a source of wisdom, truth, and inspiration. When it appears in your dreams, it may indicate you are seeking these things or that you need to seek a source of wisdom and truth so you can grow spiritually.

Other holy books or books you consider spiritual also represent the same thing in dreams. So, if there's a book by an author that has assisted in your spiritual growth, or even a work of fiction or a book of poetry, these have similar meanings to the Bible.

Blood

Our blood is our life force—we can't live without it. When we are anemic, or low on blood, we are lower in energy and vitality. Blood in dreams represents exactly this: life force energy and vitality. If you are losing blood, it suggests you feel you are losing strength or vitality in some way. If you are donating blood, it suggests you feel you are giving your life force to another. If someone else is bleeding, pay attention to what that person represents to you; it will show you which aspect of yourself you feel is draining you of life force.

Building/House

Buildings in dreams represent you. You are the building and what happens there tells you how you are feeling about you. Perhaps you are exploring many rooms, which suggests you have much to learn about yourself. Pay attention to the room you're in. For example, if you're in the kitchen, the dream may be about your need for nourishment, and being in the bathroom may be about your need to cleanse. The living or family room may represent sociability, whereas a bedroom represents rest and relaxation; an office represents industriousness, and so on.

Cancer

Cancer eats away at the body, with diseased tissue replacing healthy tissue. Likewise, cancer in your dreams represents something eating away at you and replacing the positive things in your life with negativity, or replacing things that serve you with things that don't. Cancer in a dream suggests it's time to take a deep look at yourself and remove those things taking up space in your life without producing any benefit.

In astrology, the sign Cancer is signified by the crab. It is a water sign characterized as being highly emotional. This sign is also controlled by the Moon, which represents the yin cycle, which is dark, mysterious, intuitive, and yielding. So, the zodiac sign Cancer, particularly if it's accompanied by water or crabs, suggests your dream is about being highly emotional in some way, or it may represent more yin aspects of your character.

Clothing

We wear clothing that presents a version of ourselves to the world. What we wear influences how others perceive us or how we want others to perceive us. This is what it represents in dreams as well. Pay attention to things such as the color of the clothing, shapes or patterns, the condition, etc., which offer insight about which face you are presenting to the world.

You also wear clothing as a sort of shield. When you are naked in a dream, it represents vulnerability. Clothing offers cover from feeling vulnerable, so it may also represent the ways you shield yourself from feeling too vulnerable.

Dirt/Mud

When we behave dishonorably, we might say, "I feel dirty." When we hurl insults, we call it "slinging mud." Dirt and mud represent dishonorable or dirty behavior and behaving in a way we understand on a deep level as "unclean" or unkind.

Mud can also indicate a lack of clarity; for example, if you're trying to peer through water to see what's underneath, but it's too muddy to see through, it indicates you feel unclear about something and you may not be processing your emotions well because you do not understand them.

Drugs

We call drugs a "fix," which is something we use to change how we feel quickly. In dreams, drugs signify the need for something that will quickly fix or change a situation in a way that makes it more bearable. People also take illegal drugs to duck out of the real world, so taking drugs in a dream may suggest you feel like you need to get away from the reality of your life.

Drugs also play a role in real life, often filling emotional holes. So, taking drugs in a dream may indicate you feel you're missing something emotionally in your life right now and you're trying to fill an empty emotional space.

Egg

Eggs are bundles of creative potential that can house, protect, and birth a small creature, or make a delicious breakfast. Eggs in dreams represent potential, particularly creative potential. They may also signify a desire to create or be more creative in your daily life.

Eggs in dreams can also suggest a longing to become a parent, wishing to get pregnant, or wanting to bring new life into the world in

some way. This can be literal, such as having a baby, or be figurative, such as wanting to create something new.

Food

Food represents nourishment. Pay attention to what you're eating and with whom you're eating it. Are you eating alone? This may indicate a need for solitude. Are you eating with others? This may indicate sociability. Is the food satisfying or does it leave you hungry no matter what you eat? This tells you how well you feel you are nourishing yourself in various aspects of your life. Does the food taste good or terrible? This tells you how you feel about the things you are doing to nourish yourself emotionally, creatively, or spiritually.

Ghost/Spirit

When someone in our life dies, they become a ghost or spirit. We are no longer able to reach them in the physical world. When they appear in dreams, it means we feel something in our lives, once readily accessible to us, is no longer available or reachable.

If the spirits are ghosts of people you love who have passed away, consider they might be communicating from the other side or it may

be you long to communicate in some way with them. If this is the case, communicate just as if the person is there. The communication is about you anyway, so just tell them what you need to say.

Intruder

An intruder is someone unwanted. Whether they break into our homes or try to break into our social circle, they make us feel violated because they are doing so without our consent. Intruders in dreams represent unwanted visitors as well—in this case, thoughts, beliefs, or emotions. When an intruder appears in your dreams it means something that has come into your life is unwelcome and you really don't want it there.

If you are the intruder in the dream, you may be feeling like an outsider, or you may feel like you're pushing your beliefs or desires onto another who doesn't feel the same way.

Key

Keys may open a front door, a diary, or a box full of treasure. Whatever they open, they grant us access to things not just anyone can reach. Likewise, we use keys to lock away things we don't want others to discover. In that way, keys may represent secrets and things we wish to keep hidden or protected, or they may represent access to things we deeply desire.

Keys can also represent access to new opportunities or the desire for new opportunities. If they are keys to a house or a room in a house, they may also represent unlocking some hidden portion of yourself.

Lice

We associate lice with being dirty and we also associate them with deep discomfort. Thinking about having lice often makes us squirm. Lice in dreams represent a feeling of discomfort, or even of having unclean hands and having behaved in a way that doesn't fit within our ethical framework. They may represent guilt over behaving without integrity, or suggest your behavior and choices make you deeply uncomfortable. They may also indicate something is bugging you. In that case, other context clues from the dream can help you understand what that might be.

Lightning

To be figuratively struck by lightning means sudden inspiration or recognition. Lightning in a dream may show you a sudden inspiration you have is of value, or that someone you have

met or someplace you have been is of deep value in your life. It may also indicate spiritual or emotional insight, or a breakthrough in something you've been struggling with.

Alternatively, lightning is destructive and dangerous so it could indicate danger, or that you feel something that has entered your life in a flash is highly destructive.

Money

In our society, money represents wealth, success, material gain, and status. When you dream about it, it represents these things as well. If you struggle with money in your waking life, it may also represent a deep desire for more status or success.

What money represents in dreams often depends on your personal views of money. For example, if you feel you never have enough and you struggle from paycheck to paycheck, then in a dream money may represent something you feel is unobtainable. If, however, you believe money flows to you freely and easily, it probably represents reward. Other dream symbols can help you zero in on the meaning for you.

Monster

Monsters are our deepest fears realized. When we dream of monsters, we dream of our deep, dark, hidden fears, often about ourselves. They are another manifestation of shadows that appear in our dreams, although by the time they are monsters they have grown and become almost unmanageable. Dreaming of a monster tells you it's time to face your shadows before they overcome you completely. Pay attention to the monster's characteristics, including what it looks like, how you feel about it, its coloring, etc., to get a better idea of which shadows you are avoiding.

Needle

We use sewing needles to fix tears in fabric. In dreams, a sewing needle suggests you need to "mend" something, such as a broken relationship or some hurt you're holding on to. If you're afraid of needles, they may also represent general fears.

To Freud, needles represented the phallus, so they may represent sexuality or the sex act when they appear in your dreams.

If you dream of a syringe, it is a delivery system for medication or drugs. It may also be telling you there is something in your health that needs attending to.

Rain

After it rains, the world feels clean, fresh, and new, and in dreams rain is often about renewal or the desire for cleansing or purification. It can also represent cleansing from heaven and so may indicate your desire to receive grace from a higher power. Because water also represents emotion and rain resembles tears, it can symbolize sadness or grief, or you may feel emotions are pouring down on you if the rainfall is heavy.

If the rain creates a rainbow, it suggests that, after this period, there will be reward for traveling through more difficult times.

Snow

Snow is frozen water and, as we've discussed, water in dreams represents emotions. So, snow, when it appears in dreams, represents frozen emotions. It can suggest your behavior is cold, or it may suggest you've frozen out your emotions because they feel too dark or difficult to acknowledge. When you see snow in your dreams, it is a reminder to inhabit your emotions and allow them to pass through you instead of suppressing them.

When it snows, the entire world looks clean and new, so snow can also represent peace and purity in dreams. If the snow is dirty, it suggests you feel something has marred that peace.

Teeth

Teeth in dreams are about our ability to nourish ourselves, whether physically, spiritually, financially, or emotionally. One of the most common recurring dreams people have is of their teeth falling out. These dreams expose your fears about being able to care for yourself and provide for your needs. It represents feeling a loss of personal power in some aspect of your life.

Teeth are also the last stop before words leave your mouth. When trying not to say something, we often refer to "gritting our teeth." In this way, teeth in dreams can also represent an attempt to hold back things you feel you shouldn't say.

Tidal Wave/Tsunami

Water is emotion and a tsunami is a massive wave of water that breaks over you and overwhelms you. Dreaming of a tsunami suggests you feel overwhelmed or overcome by emotion and, likely, out of control. It may also suggest it is time to allow yourself to feel whatever emotion you've suppressed so it doesn't become overwhelming. By allowing and expressing the emotion, you can clear it instead of keeping it deep inside where it can ultimately do harm.

Train

Like other vehicles, trains are about your journey along life's path. Trains run along a track; if the train stays on the track, it suggests your life is following the right path, and if it derails, it may suggest you're following a path that doesn't serve your greatest good. A dream with a runaway train may suggest that you feel out of control.

Perhaps not surprisingly, Freud saw trains as another symbol for the phallus, so trains may also represent sexuality or sexual desire. Freud saw a train entering a tunnel as symbolic of coitus.

Twins

Twins have the same meanings as the number two; they may represent opposites such as yin and yang or duality. However, if the number two has appeared in the form of people, pay attention to the clothing they wear and other things about them to gain deeper insight into your dream's meaning.

In Western astrology, twins represent the sign of Gemini, which is an air sign ruled by Mercury. The twins of Gemini can have both negative and positive expression. Negatively expressed they may represent duplicity or being two-faced. Positively expressed they can represent balance and equanimity. These are both possible meanings of twins in dreams.

Water

In dreams, water always represents emotions. Calm water represents peaceful emotions. Choppy water represents more turbulent emotions. Clear water suggests you clearly understand your emotions. Murky water suggests you are hiding your emotions, even from yourself, or that you can't see them clearly.

In Taoist philosophy, the water element is yin (feminine, mysterious, yielding), but with elements of yang (active, unyielding, aggressive, masculine). So, water, depending on its form in the dream, may also represent various emotional aspects of yin and yang. For example, a raging river is a yang form of water. Its aggressive action shapes the land around it. A lake, on the other hand, is a yin form of water; it is passive and still. Boiling water is yang; cool water is yin, and so on. Water's expression in a dream is essential to understanding the emotions it represents.

Zombie

Zombies are the walking dead. They are bodies without emotions or brains, filled only with the desire to feed without any thought for consequences. Seeing a zombie in a dream suggests you feel dead in some aspect of your life, usually emotionally although sometimes spiritually. You may be living and thinking without allowing yourself to stop and feel your emotions, or you may be pursuing some aim so aggressively you've forgotten to stop and consider the effect on others. If you're being pursued by a zombie, it may suggest you feel another's desire is consuming you without thought for your feelings, needs, or desires.

PLOT/ACTION

A dream's plot is how you pull the dream all together. It helps you understand how the context, people, and symbols all come together into a coherent whole. As with other entries in this dream dictionary, however, personal experience, filters, and belief systems will alter the definitions somewhat. Look to personal meaning first.

Alien/UFO Encounter

Alien and UFO encounters in dreams mean you feel alienated or that you have alienated someone. You may feel as though you are on the outside looking in. It can also mean you have alienated some part of yourself—it's another form of a shadow dream. The alien is pointing out the "alien" part of yourself that longs for recognition.

These dreams also often occur when you're in a new situation that feels unfamiliar, such as a new job, a new school, or in a new relationship. In these cases, the dream reveals that you still feel uncomfortable and a bit like an outsider.

Space creatures in dreams may also be representations of feeling a little "spacey" yourself, suggesting you feel disconnected from yourself, have your head in the clouds, or the like.

Being Late

When you are late to something, it means time is running or has run out. When the plot of your dream involves being late or the fear of being late, it's a representation that you feel time is running out on something significant in your life and you're anxious or stressed about it. It may also show you don't feel ready for something that is rapidly approaching. This is a manifestation of anxiety in dreams.

Being Lost

When you're lost, you feel confused and don't know which way to turn. When a dream plot involves being lost, it means you don't really know where to go from here, or you might feel aimless or undirected. If you lose something in a dream, then the object you lose will tell you which aspect of your life feels aimless or directionless.

If someone else is lost, it suggests you feel like you are "losing" that person or that person is moving in a different direction from you and you worry the relationship is slipping away.

Birth/Breastfeeding

Even men can have dreams about giving birth and/or breastfeeding. Often, these two dream elements show up in the same plot. Dreams about giving birth are about creativity and finding new directions in life. Alternatively, it could be about your desire to have children or build a family. Breastfeeding is about nurturing your creation, or it could be about nurturing your innocence. When this is your dream's plot, it suggests you are coming up on a new beginning or period of creativity, or it may suggest you desire greater creativity in your life. Breastfeeding your creation suggests you have a strong desire to nurture.

Break In

If the plot of your dream is about a robbery, burglary, or break in, pay attention to whether you're the one breaking in or someone is breaking into your place. When you dream you're the burglar breaking in somewhere, it suggests you are looking for something significant, usually something buried in your subconscious. If someone else is attempting a break in, it means the subconscious something you are denying is trying to break through to your conscious mind. If someone is breaking into your house, it suggests you may feel vulnerable or unsafe emotionally.

Breakup

Breakups are about letting go. When the plot of your dream is about a breakup with someone, it suggests it's time to let go of something you're holding on to. It can also be about endings of any kind, suggesting something is coming to an end. The other symbols in the dream and the dream's context will help you understand what it is you need to let go of or what is ending.

Dreaming about breaking up with your significant other can also show your true feelings about that relationship. For example, if you dream your spouse is divorcing you and you are devastated, it suggests the relationship is still very important to you. On the other hand, if your attitude is, "Okay, cool," it may suggest the relationship has run its course and it's time to move on.

Can't Find Car/Stolen Vehicle

Vehicles represent your path in life and a common dream many people have is that their car is lost or stolen. This dream suggests you feel like you've lost your way; you have wandered off your life's path and don't know how to get back to it. Being unable to find your vehicle, which represents your path, means you may be feeling aimless or directionless. If the car is stolen, it suggests you feel like something outside of yourself has pulled you away from your path in life. It may also suggest you are struggling with some type of an identity crisis or existential crisis in your waking life.

Can't Move/Paralyzed

This isn't always a symbol, although sometimes it is. Your body actually experiences a condition called sleep paralysis during REM sleep so you can't act out your dreams. Sometimes, people wake partially from dreams, but their body is still unable to move for a second or two. If this happens to you, you may think you're dreaming you can't move, when it's actually true that you can't move.

Alternatively, if it's symbolic paralysis within the dream, you may feel a sense of being stuck or an inability to deal with certain situations in your life. The context and symbols of the dream will provide more clues.

Car Accident

Vehicles represent your path in life and crashing one suggests you feel overwhelmed and are afraid you may be headed for a physical, spiritual, or emotional crash. The dream may also be telling you it's time to proceed more cautiously on your life's path and carefully reconsider your choices to make sure they serve your highest good. Alternatively, it may suggest you're afraid you're on the wrong path and are headed for a collision. If someone else is driving and crashes the car you're both in, it may indicate you are out of control and some shadow aspect of yourself is in the driver's seat, steering you toward disaster.

Chasing/Being Chased

Chasing or being chased is among the most common dream plots and they often arise in recurring dreams. When you are being chased in a dream, it suggests you are running from something. It could be some shadow aspect of yourself, an emotion, or even a responsibility. Pay attention to what is chasing you and the dream's context to understand what you're avoiding.

If you're the chaser, it suggests you're reaching for or pursuing something that feels just out of your grasp. Notice how close you are to what you're trying to catch to get an

idea of how close you feel you are to your goal. Additionally, notice what you're chasing and how you feel about it as well as the context of the dream to understand what goals or ambitions the dream is revealing.

Cheating/Infidelity

Infidelity dreams are very common. If you're with someone in your dream who is not your current partner, but you're not really aware in the dream world that you're cheating, it isn't actually an infidelity dream. It's a dream about loving the aspect of yourself the person you're with represents.

If, however, you recognize your behavior in the dream as infidelity, it is telling you something about the state of your current relationship. The dream suggests you are dissatisfied with your current partner, or you feel there are real issues in the relationship that need to be resolved. If you are not currently partnered, it may suggest you need to heal your relationship with yourself.

Crying

There's not a lot of mystery to what crying means in a dream. Just as crying when you're awake allows you to express and release emotions, crying in a dream represents you releasing emotions. It may be helping you process current grief or sadness you're not acknowledging or dealing with while awake. If you dream someone else is crying, pay attention to who it is and what they represent to you; it will tell you which emotions or aspects of yourself you need to tune in to in order to express negative emotions in a healthy way.

Crying can also represent cleansing and purification.

Death

Death dreams are super freaky, but they aren't quite as horrible as they might seem. Death is about endings, which inevitably lead to new beginnings. For example, if the plot of a dream is that you die, it's a sign that some aspect of your life is ending, but something new will begin. The dream is of completion and closure so you can move on. In the tarot deck, Death is a major archetype that represents bringing something to an end to facilitate a new beginning as well.

If you dream someone else dies, pay attention to who it is. That person will represent some aspect of yourself and the dream means it's time to bring that aspect to completion.

Dreaming of killing or murdering means you wish to kill some aspect of yourself because you dislike it or have disowned it. This is a manifestation of a shadow dream.

Driving

Plots about driving are about your journey through life. Pay attention to how you feel. Are you in control or out of control? Are you relaxed or stressed? Joyful or angry? These all tell you how you feel your journey is going. If you're not driving and someone else is, it indicates either you feel the aspect of you that person represents is in control right now, or you feel you're not in control of your life's path. Pay attention to context and other symbols to determine who or what you might feel is driving you right now.

Drowning

Water is always about emotion in dreams, and dreaming that you're drowning suggests you feel completely overwhelmed. If someone else is drowning in your dreams, notice what that person represents to you. What is your primary emotion when you think of that person? Chances are, that's the emotion that's overwhelming you. Pay attention to context and symbols to understand more about how or why you feel like you're drowning in emotion.

Drowning in dreams may also indicate you feel the need to "come up for air." In other words, your life just may be busy, stressful, and overwhelming right now and the dream is reminding you it's time to slow down and breathe.

Earthquake

Just as earthquakes shake up parts of the planet, dreams where earthquakes are the plot suggest some kind of a shake-up in your life. And just as you are unable to control an actual earthquake, when they are the plot of a dream, it suggests you feel you have no control of whatever it is shaking you up.

For some people who are geo sensitive (meaning they have the ability to sense earthquakes before they happen), earthquake dreams may be prophetic. If you notice you have earthquake dreams and, within a day or two, an earthquake occurs, these dreams may be prophetic and you may be geo sensitive.

Eating

Dream plots about eating are about nourishment and fulfillment. This can be physical nourishment, but it's more likely about spiritual, mental, social, and emotional nourishment. Notice whether you're enjoying the food and if it satiates you or leaves you wanting more. Does it taste good or bad? If you're eating alone, you may feel you need social nourishment; you might be lonely and longing for companionship or friendship, for example.

For people with food issues and eating disorders, eating in dreams may represent anxiety. For example, I have celiac disease and one of my common recurring dreams is that I accidentally eat gluten. This dream represents my anxiety about nourishing myself emotionally, physically, spiritually, or in some other aspect in the "wrong" way.

Experiment

In waking life, experiments are something we do to explore possibilities and principles. In a dream plot, the experiment represents a sense of exploration and discovery. These dreams may suggest you are ready to try something new and exciting or it may prompt you to explore new ideas, philosophies, and possibilities.

If you are the subject of an experiment, it suggests you feel at the mercy of something or someone else, or you might feel as if you are "under a microscope," being watched carefully.

Falling

Falling is one of the most common dream plots. There's a myth that if you hit the ground in a falling dream, you'll die in real life, but that's untrue. I've hit the ground in a falling dream more than once and lived to tell about it.

However, falling dreams are dreams about anxiety and lack of control. When you fall, it starts with an uncontrolled action (in other words, you didn't initiate the fall), and you also have no control over how you land. In dreams, falling signifies you feel you lack control in some aspect of your life or that you currently don't have a safe place to land; that is, you don't feel safe or secure.

Finding Money or Treasure

Some dreams offer encouragement and inspiration—and that includes dreams about finding money or treasure. These dreams may suggest there is something worthy within you that you will discover, or they may indicate your efforts will soon be rewarded. Dreams with this plot

often come when you've been working hard at something, but the rewards aren't necessarily financial. For example, a payoff for hard work may be a stronger relationship, a healthier body, a promotion at work, or even the realization of a long-held dream. These dreams encourage you to keep going, letting you know you've almost reached the finish line and your efforts have been worth it.

Fire

Metaphorically, fire represents passion, anger, jealousy, or some other powerful emotion. It has all these meanings when it appears as a plot in dreams. When something is on fire, it suggests some powerful emotion or passion is burning hotly right now. Dreaming in this way can help these emotions pass through you instead of allowing them to control you. If your house is burning, remember that your house represents you, so it suggests your overwhelmingly passionate emotions are causing damage. Alternatively, fire can represent purification, the need for purification, or the desire for a new beginning.

Flood

Floods come from an uncontrollable excess of water. As we've discussed, water represents emotion. So, if your dream plot is about a flood, it suggests you feel your emotions are out of control and overtaking your life. Flood dreams are similar to tsunami dreams in that they signify your emotions are deep, overwhelming, and possibly too much to handle right now. It can also suggest you feel you are overwhelming others with your needs or emotions in your waking life.

Flying

Flying dreams are a common positive dream. They represent freedom, reaching for and achieving goals, and soaring to new heights. Flying can also show you a new perspective, because when you fly you see the world in a way you don't while on Earth. Likewise, because we conflate heaven with being above us and in the sky, flying may represent spiritual seeking and/or attainment or enlightenment. Notice how you feel when you fly. Does it feel exhilarating or terrifying? If terrifying, it may suggest you're afraid to reach for your goals.

Getting Shot

If you dream of being shot, pay attention to who shot you. What does that person represent to you? Being shot by someone in a dream indicates you are feeling upset or ashamed about some aspect of yourself—probably the aspect represented by the person shooting you. If you shoot someone, again, ask what that person represents. Shooting them represents you trying to eliminate that aspect of self from your personality. If someone shoots you and misses, or you shoot and miss, it suggests your aim is off and you need to reconsider certain goals and aspirations.

Going Bald/Losing Hair

Dreams about going bald represent feelings of insecurity. Losing your hair in your dream suggests you are worried about your physical attractiveness or personal power and is often associated with aging. If you deliberately remove your hair in a dream, it may have a more spiritual meaning, suggesting spiritual cleansing and growth.

Like clothing, hair can also represent the social mask we present to the world. Losing your hair in a dream may also suggest you feel vulnerable and exposed or that you are putting down your mask and showing your true nature.

Hiding

In waking life, when we hide, we are keeping others from finding us. In dreams when we hide, it suggests we are hiding aspects of ourselves we don't want others to discover. If someone is hiding from you in a dream, you may feel others are keeping vital aspects of themselves hidden from you. If you're hiding an object, then you may be trying to hide whatever that object symbolizes. For example, hiding a glass of water might represent hiding your emotions, whereas hiding a key may suggest you're locking away access to important aspects of yourself from another person.

Injury

If you are injured in a dream, it means you feel someone or something has hurt you or that you have hurt someone else. Injuries in dreams may also suggest old unhealed wounds, with the dream telling you it is time to deal with and release them so you no longer carry the pain in your life and allow it to affect you. Context clues and other symbols can help you understand what wounds or injuries it is time to deal with. For example, if you are wounded in the chest, it may be suggesting

it's time to deal with hurts you are carrying around from a love relationship.

Kidnapped

Someone who is kidnapped is taken and held against their will. In dreams, the meaning is similar: It suggests you feel you are being kept from something or someone important, such as an aspiration or creative idea. You may be feeling manipulated or controlled by another. If you kidnap someone, it suggests you feel you may be holding someone else back from their goals or aspirations or that you are forcing someone to see things the way you want them to instead of allowing them to develop their own ideas and opinions, or you may be behaving in a manipulative and controlling manner toward others.

Killing/Murder

Dreams where you murder or kill someone—or where someone is trying to murder or kill you—are highly disturbing. They almost always suggest you wish to kill off some aspect of yourself, usually a shadow aspect but not always. For example, if you are openly naive and you're killing a baby, it may suggest your naivety isn't serving your greatest good anymore and it's time to allow that to go. Pay attention to who

and what is being killed and then look up the symbolism for that and it will tell you what parts of yourself you wish to be rid of.

If you see a killer in your dreams who is killing others and you're not involved, then it suggests you've cut off (killed) some vital aspect of yourself that you still need. Look to context and other symbols to determine what that might be.

Kissing

Kissing has many meanings in society—from love and romance to respect and fidelity. It has similar meanings in dreams. For example, if you're kissing someone's hand, it may suggest you feel deeply respectful. If you're kissing a ring, it may suggest you wish to pledge fidelity.

If you're engaging in romantic kissing, it may suggest you desire romance or you need to bring more romance into your current relationship.

If you're kissing a baby, it may be that it's time to nurture your innocence and creativity.

In general, kissing is a positive sign that shows love, affection, and respect and it has these same meanings in your dreams. Pay attention to who you're kissing, where, and how you feel about it for more information.

Losing Something

When you lose things in dreams, it often suggests the same thing as in the waking world—that you need to be more organized and systematic in your approach to life. The dream may indicate it's time to declutter and reorganize your home, for example.

You may also have dreams of losing something when you've experienced a big life change. For example, the year my dad died, I dreamed constantly of losing my car (the symbol for my path in life). In retrospect it's easy to see that those dreams were telling me I felt I'd lost my way in the wake of his death. My dreams were a way of coping with my grief and loss.

Making a Discovery

Discovering something in your dreams suggests you have found some new interest, passion, or aspect of yourself in your waking life. This may be some aspect of your subconscious self or shadow, or it may be a new skill or a new aspiration or goal you didn't realize you had. These dreams are positive and are a great form of guidance, encouraging you to pursue this new discovery because it will serve your greatest good. What you find or discover in your dream can tell you what it is in your waking life.

Malfunctioning Technology

In today's world, we use technology as our main source of communication. When technology malfunctions in a dream, it suggests you feel you are not communicating well or are not receiving someone else's messages. For example, if you're on a cell phone and can't hear what the other person is saying, it suggests you either are not listening or not hearing the meaning of what they are trying to tell you. Malfunctioning technology dreams encourage you to communicate more clearly and effectively and to listen more carefully.

Alternatively, these dreams can suggest you feel you're not being heard or not being communicated with effectively.

Marriage

Just as marriage represents a happy partnership and unity of two disparate parts in waking life, it represents the same thing when you're asleep. However, it doesn't necessarily signify a romantic partnership, although it could. It could indicate a partnership with self, for example, joining together your

shadow and conscious selves into a more complete whole, or it could indicate it's time to enter into a partnership to meet important goals and aspirations.

Marriage dreams are often about bringing together your dual self—the yin (feminine, dark, mysterious, yielding, passive) and the yang (masculine, aggressive, light, active) parts of yourself. It encourages you to recognize that neither half of the duality is either good or bad and that both poles exist to create a harmonious whole.

Meeting Someone Famous

When you dream of meeting someone famous, the dream meaning will be individual to you because it depends on who the celebrity is and what they represent to you. For example, if you dream of meeting a celebrity you idolize, it could be about optimizing those aspects of yourself that the celebrity reminds you of. If the celebrity is someone you find shallow and vain or dislike, then it may be about the aspects of yourself you wish to disown. Ask yourself, who is this person and what do they mean to me?

Celebrities often embody archetypes in dreams, so see if you can match them to one of the archetypes. If the celebrity is a religious figure, such as Jesus, Muhammad, or Buddha, then the dream may be about spiritual aspirations or guidance.

Moving House

Dreams about moving from one home to another are about change and, often, the desire for change. Because your house represents you, pay attention to the features of the new house. What is different? This can tell you what you wish to change.

If you're moving from an apartment to a house, it may suggest you are ready to move into a more permanent situation in some aspect of your life. If you're moving from a house into an apartment, it may suggest you desire to move into a transitional phase. Moving from a hotel to a house suggests you're ready to transition to something new such as a new spiritual path or career path.

Naked/Underwear

Walking around naked or in your underwear in public is probably the number one dream I'm asked about. These dreams are almost always about feeling exposed and vulnerable. Without clothing, you expose yourself to the

world and allow others to see you without your mask. Where you are, who is there, and how you feel will give you more information about where you're feeling vulnerable or exposed and why. The dream can either be about true feelings of vulnerability or fear of vulnerability and exposure.

Natural Disaster

There are many kinds of natural disasters and each has its own meaning. However, in general, natural disasters shake the foundations of our lives and are beyond our control. So, when they occur in dreams, they suggest we are feeling shaken up and out of control, often by something over which we feel we have no say. For example, if the natural disaster is water related, it's likely about emotions. If it's mud related, it may be about lack of clarity or feeling unclean. If it's a volcano, it may mean you feel some hot passion or emotion, such as jealousy or anger, which is out of control and taking over your life.

Packing

When we pack in our waking lives, it means something is changing. In dreams it means the same. Packing signifies you have big changes ahead and that you are removing the things that won't serve the change to make way for things that will.

If you keep packing and packing but can never finish, or there's so much to pack you don't know how you'll finish, it may suggest you're feeling a bit overwhelmed by the upcoming changes and unsure how you'll handle them, or you may feel trepidation at making way for something new, no matter how exciting it might be.

Plane Crash

If you have a phobia of flying, then the meaning of this dream is likely a no-brainer: it's a manifestation of your anxiety about flying. However, if you don't fear flying, it may mean something else.

Airplanes represent goals and ambitions, so to see one crash in a dream suggests you're worried you're aiming too high or you fear you will crash and not reach those goals. These dreams can be about self-doubt or they may be about being overly confident and suggest you need to move cautiously toward your goals with eyes open lest you crash.

Pregnant

Pregnancy dreams are about creativity and growth. Even men can have pregnancy dreams, although it is far less common than for women. These dreams suggest you are incubating a creative idea and you desire deeply for it to grow to fruition. If you give birth in the dream, it suggests you are ready to bring your creative idea into the world.

Of course, pregnancy dreams can also be about a desire to have children, or they may be about being pregnant. For example, you may dream you are pregnant before you know you are because sometimes the body has its own wisdom and you are subconsciously aware of it before your conscious mind knows. Likewise, if you dream about your pregnancy while you're pregnant, these dreams are often either processing dreams or dreams associated with common worries pregnant mothers have.

Running

In dreams, the direction you're running can help you understand the meaning of the dream. For example, if you are running away from something, it suggests you wish to get away from something in your waking life, or that something is no longer serving you. If you're running toward something, it suggests you are ready for change and welcoming something new in your life, or that you're heading for your goals at a steady clip. If you're running because you're being chased, it suggests you're trying to escape an inevitable truth about yourself. If you're running for fitness, it may be your body telling you it needs more exercise.

Swimming

Swimming brings us back to water. Water is emotion; swimming is how you move through the emotions. For example, if you are scuba diving you may be exploring your emotions.

As with running, pay attention to the direction you are swimming. Are you swimming away from something? This suggests an emotion you are trying to escape or wish to leave behind. Are you swimming toward something? This suggests an emotion you're trying to find and integrate. Are you swimming in circles around something? This suggests an emotion you are circling and observing but not yet ready to approach. Are you swimming back and forth between two things? This suggests you are moving between two emotions and can't decide which one to stick with.

Taking a Test

Just as you take tests academically to assess your progress, taking a test in dreams suggests you are either being tested or assessing yourself in some way. If you're taking a test on a subject you know nothing about, you may feel as though you're in over your head in some aspect of your life or you need to learn more about something important. If you fail, it can pinpoint aspects of your life about which you feel insecure. If you ace the test, it suggests you feel ready to meet any of life's challenges head-on.

Teeth Falling Out

The reason your teeth fall out can tell you more about the meaning of this type of dream. However, as discussed earlier, teeth typically represent our ability to nourish ourselves in some way, or our ability to hold in our words when they are unkind or unneeded. So, to understand what it means when teeth fall out in your dream, pay attention to why. If they fall out because they're rotted, it suggests you feel you haven't been living up to your values or ethics. If someone punches them out, it suggests you have been unkind in your words or thoughts. If they fall out in front of others, it may suggest you are afraid others will see you are not living up to your personal standards.

Throwing Up/Vomiting

When you vomit, your body is ridding itself of something that can cause greater illness. In dreams, vomiting has a similar meaning. It suggests you wish to (or need to) rid yourself of something not serving your greatest good or that is poisoning you. This can be literal, such as something you eat, or it could be figurative and symbolic, such as ideas, thoughts, or attitudes. Vomiting in a dream means it's time to let go of things that not only don't serve you but that also can harm you if you continue to hold on to them.

Trapped

Feeling trapped translates almost literally in your dreams. If you dream you are trapped, chances are you feel "trapped" or stuck in some aspect of your life. Pay attention to where you're trapped. For example, if you're trapped in the basement, you may be feeling constricted by your shadow-self. If you're trapped in a school, you may feel restricted by a lack of education or knowledge about something. If you're trapped at a doctor's office, some aspect of your health may be making you feel stuck. If you're trapped in a closet, you may be feeling constricted because you have been unwilling to allow some aspect of yourself to rise to the surface.

If you're the one setting the trap, it may suggest you want to continue to hold on to things that no longer serve you.

Travel/Vacation

Sometimes dreaming of travel or a vacation simply means you need to relax, or you need a vacation. It can also be about an upcoming trip you are planning to take. Symbolically, traveling also suggests you are ready to embark upon a new path, find a new goal, or try something new in your life. It can also represent a longing for excitement, the wish for a change of scenery, or the desire to have new experiences. Where you go, who you're with, and your mode of transportation can all provide deeper clues about what you'd like to change or experience.

For example, I once had a dream I was traveling to Hawaii (which is not unusual, because my sister lives there) on an airplane, and when we landed, we were greeted by dolphins and orca whales. In the context of that dream, I realized I had higher spiritual aspirations and was longing for a change. Shortly thereafter, I switched from my career as a corporate marketing communications specialist writing about operator interface terminals (exciting, huh?) to full-time writer writing about spiritual and metaphysical topics.

Unable to Scream

This is another common dream. Something terrifying is happening, so you open your mouth to scream and nothing comes out. This is almost always a dream about not feeling heard or feeling like you are holding back important aspects of yourself.

This can also be related to sleep paralysis (see page 55), which about 40 percent of the population will experience at some point in their life. If you wake in the act of screaming in the dream, you may have remnants of the dream where you believed you couldn't scream in the dream when actually it was your body unable to complete the action due to sleep paralysis.

War/Nuclear War

Just as wars are conflict in the real world, they signify internal conflict in your dream life. These dreams often suggest your emotions or other aspects of your life feel chaotic and you feel at odds with yourself or others. War dreams may suggest your anger is out of control, for instance, or something else is causing significant conflict in your life so you feel like you're fighting all the time.

War dreams can be about aggression as well. If you're feeling angry or aggressive about something in your life, it will often manifest as a war dream.

Nuclear war is especially destructive. It may be a warning that your negativity and chaos are quickly approaching a point of no return where you may create destruction so deep you can't take it back. It shows that it's important to rein it in and deal with your negative emotions before you pass that point of no return.

RESOURCES

The following resources may be helpful in your dream interpretation.

WEBSITES

Dream Moods (dreammoods.com): I find this to be the most comprehensive online dream dictionary and the one that is the closest in its symbolism to what I understand dream symbols to mean.

LoveToKnow Feng Shui (feng-shui.lovetoknow.com): Here you'll find excellent explanations about Taoist philosophy including yin and yang, which I reference quite a bit in the dream symbols.

LoveToKnow Horoscopes (horoscopes.lovetoknow.com): You'll find symbolism here for Chinese astrology and Western astrology as well as archetypes and tarot symbolism, all of which are helpful for dream interpretation.

BOOKS

Dreams & Visions by Edgar Cayce

The Interpretation of Dreams by Sigmund Freud, translated by A. A. Brill

Jungian Dream Interpretation by James A. Hall

Man and His Symbols by Carl G. Jung

The Meaning of Dreams by Calvin S. Hall, Jr.

DREAM DICTIONARIES

The Book of Psychic Symbols by Melanie Barnum

Dream Dictionary for Dummies by Penney Peirce

The Dream Interpretation Dictionary by J. M. DeBord

Llewellyn's Complete Dictionary of Dreams by Michael Lennox

12,000 *Dreams Interpreted* by Gustavus Hindman Miller, Linda Shields, and Lenore Skomal

REFERENCES

al-'Awlaki, Anwar. "17 Rules of Islamic Dream Interpretations." *The Muslim Times*. March 19, 2018. www.themuslimtimes.info/2018/03/19/17-rules-of-islamic-dream-interpretations/.

Ancient Origins. "The Egyptian Dream Book." *Ancient Origins*. May 4, 2014. www.ancient-origins .net/myths-legends/egyptian-dream-book-001621.

Bahadur, Tulika. "Gudea's Dreams." *On Art and Aesthetics*. January 7, 2016. www.onartandaesthetics .com/2016/01/07/gudeas-dreams/.

Berman, Ruth. "Activation-Synthesis Theory." *REM Sleep*. www.macalester.edu/projects/ubnrp /website_rem_sleep/dreamActivationSynthesis.html.

Breus, Michael J. "Why Do We Dream?" *Psychology Today*. February 13, 2015. www.psychology today.com/us/blog/sleep-newzzz/201502/why-do-we-dream.

Brown, Chip. "The Stubborn Scientist Who Unraveled a Mystery of the Night." *Smithsonian.com*. October 2003. www.smithsonianmag.com/science-nature/the-stubborn-scientist-who-unraveled -a-mystery-of-the-night-91514538/.

Cai, Denise J., et al. "REM, Not Incubation, Improves Creativity by Priming Associative Networks." *Proceedings of the National Academy of Sciences of the United States of America* 106, no. 25 (June 23, 2009): 10130–10134. doi:10.1073/pnas.0900271106.

Crisp, Tony. "Ancient Greece—Dream Beliefs." *Dream Hawk*. www.dreamhawk.com/dream -encyclopedia/ancient-greece-dream-beliefs/.

"Dreams and Dream Interpretation." *Edgar Cayce's A.R.E.* www.edgarcayce.org/the-readings /dreams/.

Foulkes, David. "Dreaming and Consciousness." *European Journal of Cognitive Psychology*, 8 (November 2007): 39–55. doi.org/10.1080/09541449008406196.

Freud, Sigmund. *The Interpretation of Dreams*. Independently published, 2017.

Hall, Calvin S. *The Meaning of Dreams*. New York: McGraw-Hill, 1966.

Hamori, Esther J., and Jonathan Stökl. *Perchance to Dream: Dream Divination in the Bible and the Ancient Near East*. Atlanta: SBL Press, 2018.

Hobson, J. A., and R. W. McCarley. "The Brain as a Dream State Generator: An Activation-Synthesis Hypothesis of the Dream Process." *The American Journal of Psychiatry* 134, no. 12 (December 1977): 1335–48. doi:10.1176/ajp.134.12.1335.

Hoffman, C. "Dumuzi's Dream: Dream Analysis in Ancient Mesopotamia." *Dreaming* 14, no. 4 (2004): 240–251. dx.doi.org/10.1037/1053-0797.14.4.240.

Hurd, Ryan. "The Dream Theories of Carl Jung." *Dream Studies Portal*. www.dreamstudies.org /2009/11/25/carl-jung-dream-interpretation/.

"Insights from Dreams." *Edgar Cayce's A.R.E.* www.edgarcayce.org/the-readings/dreams /insights-from-dreams/.

Kappler, Kevin. "Dream Interpretation in Ancient Greece: Artemidorus Oneirocritica." *GoMentor*. April 30, 2014. https://www.gomentor.com/articles/ Dream-Interpretation-in-Ancient-Greece-Artemidorus-Oneirocritica-23538.

Kresser, Chris. "How Artificial Light Is Wrecking Your Sleep, and What to Do about It." *Chris Kresser* (blog). Chriskresser.com. April 1 2019. chriskresser.com/how-artificial-light-is -wrecking-your-sleep-and-what to do-about-it/.

McNamara, Patrick. "Visitation Dreams." *Psychology Today*. October 8, 2011. www.psychology today.com/us/blog/dream-catcher/201110/visitation-dreams.

"Morpheus." *Greek Gods & Goddesses*. June 11, 2018. www.greekgodsandgoddesses.net/gods /morpheus/.

National Sleep Foundation. "How Often Do We Dream?" National Sleep Foundation. www.sleep.org/articles/how-often-dreams/.

Psychology Today. "Motivated Reasoning." *Psychology Today*. www.psychologytoday.com/us /basics/motivated-reasoning.

Rettner, Rachael. "Scientists Can Now Tell If Someone Is Dreaming from Their Brain Waves." *LiveScience*. April 11, 2017. www.livescience.com/58646-brain-waves-dreaming.html.

Schneider, Adam, and G. William Domhoff. "Dreams FAQ." University of California Santa Barbara. www2.ucsc.edu/dreams/FAQ/.

"Sleep Paralysis." rev. Sabrina M. Felson. WebMD. October 26, 2018. www.webmd.com /sleep-disorders/guide/sleep-paralysis#1-2.

Stratos, Anita. "Egypt: Perchance to Dream: Dreams and Their Meaning in Ancient Egypt." *Tour Egypt*. www.touregypt.net/featurestories/dream.html.

Tavris, Carol, and Elliot Aronson. *Mistakes Were Made (but Not by Me): Why We Justify Foolish Beliefs, Bad Decisions, and Hurtful Acts*. London: Pinter & Martin Ltd., 2015.

Taylor, Marjorie, et al. "Imaginary Worlds in Middle Childhood: A Qualitative Study of Two Pairs of Coordinated Paracosms." *Creativity Research Journal* 27, no. 2 (June 11, 2015): 167–174. doi.org/10.1080/10400419.2015.1030318.

Timm, Leo. "How the Chinese Explained Dreams." *The Epoch Times*. June 10, 2015. www.the epochtimes.com/how-the-chinese-explained-dreams_1384033.html.

United Church of God. "Does God Communicate with Christians Through Dreams Today? Do My Dreams Have Spiritual Significance?" *United Church of God*. www.ucg.org/bible-study-tools /bible-questions-and-answers/does-god-communicate-with-christians-through-dreams.

Vincent, Alice. "Yesterday: The Song That Started as Scrambled Eggs." *The Telegraph*. June 18, 2015. www.telegraph.co.uk/culture/music/the-beatles/11680415/Yesterday-the-song-that-started -as-Scrambled-Eggs.html.

Wamsley, Erin J., and Robert Stickgold. "Dreaming and Offline Memory Processing." *Current Biology* 20, no. 23 (December 7, 2010): R1010–R1013. doi:10.1016/j.cub.2010.10.045.

INDEX

ACKNOWLEDGMENTS

Throughout my life and career, I've been blessed with many beautiful souls who have played key roles in my path as a writer and human being. Without them, my life would be very different.

I'd like to thank first and foremost my family both of origin and of choice; my mom, dad, and sisters, my husband, Jim, and sons Tanner and Kevin, and all of my chosen family of fabulous friends; there are too many to name, and I'm afraid I'd forget someone. Their support has always been unwavering and I am grateful. Thanks also to Cheryl Knight and Chad Wilson, who gave my dream interpretation column a home at *Paranormal Underground* magazine, as well as to all who have shared their dreams with me in columns, classes, and private conversations over the years. I'm honored you've allowed me a glimpse into the world of your dreams.

Finally, I'd also like to thank everyone at Callisto Media, especially those who helped create this book including Nana Twumasi, Mary Cassells, Kristen Finello, and the many others who have been instrumental in turning my humble words into a work to be proud of.

ABOUT THE AUTHOR

Karen Frazier is the author of books about metaphysics, crystal healing, energy healing, dream interpretation, and the paranormal. As a professional writer, she has ghostwritten a number of books and penned hundreds of articles about a variety of topics.

Karen is a columnist for *Paranormal Underground* magazine. She currently writes two columns for the magazine: Dreams and Symbols, and Metaphysics and Energy Healing. For more than seven years, Karen was the co-host of Paranormal Underground Radio, and she formerly served as *Paranormal Underground*'s managing editor. She is also the Paranormal and Horoscopes editor for LoveToKnow and she writes feng shui, numerology, palmistry, psychic phenomena, paranormal, divination, and tarot articles for the site.

An intuitive energy healer who is a Usui Reiki Ryoho Master-Teacher (*Shinpiden*), Karen is also a Raku-Kai Reiki Master, a Karuna Ki Reiki Master, a Crystal Reiki Master, and a certified animal Usui Reiki Ryoho practitioner as well as an ordained minister for the International Metaphysical Ministry. She has extensively studied and taken professional level courses in numerous energy, alternative healing, metaphysical, dream interpretation, and divination techniques and concepts.

Karen holds a Bachelor of Metaphysical Science (BMSc) and a Master of Metaphysical Science (MMSc) as well as a PhD in Metaphysical Parapsychology. She is currently working on her doctoral dissertation focusing on sound as a source of spiritual healing in order to earn her Doctor of Divinity (DD) in Spiritual Healing.

Printed in the USA
CPSIA information can be obtained
at www.ICGtesting.com
CBHW040511010224
3921CB00002B/22